Geometric, Abstract and Mandalas Coloring Book

Loretta Emmons

Dedication

This book is dedicated to my husband for his continued support and love. Also dedicated to everyone who still loves to color!

Acknowledgments

Thanks to Pixabay for a plethora of pictures I was able to transform into this amazing coloring book.

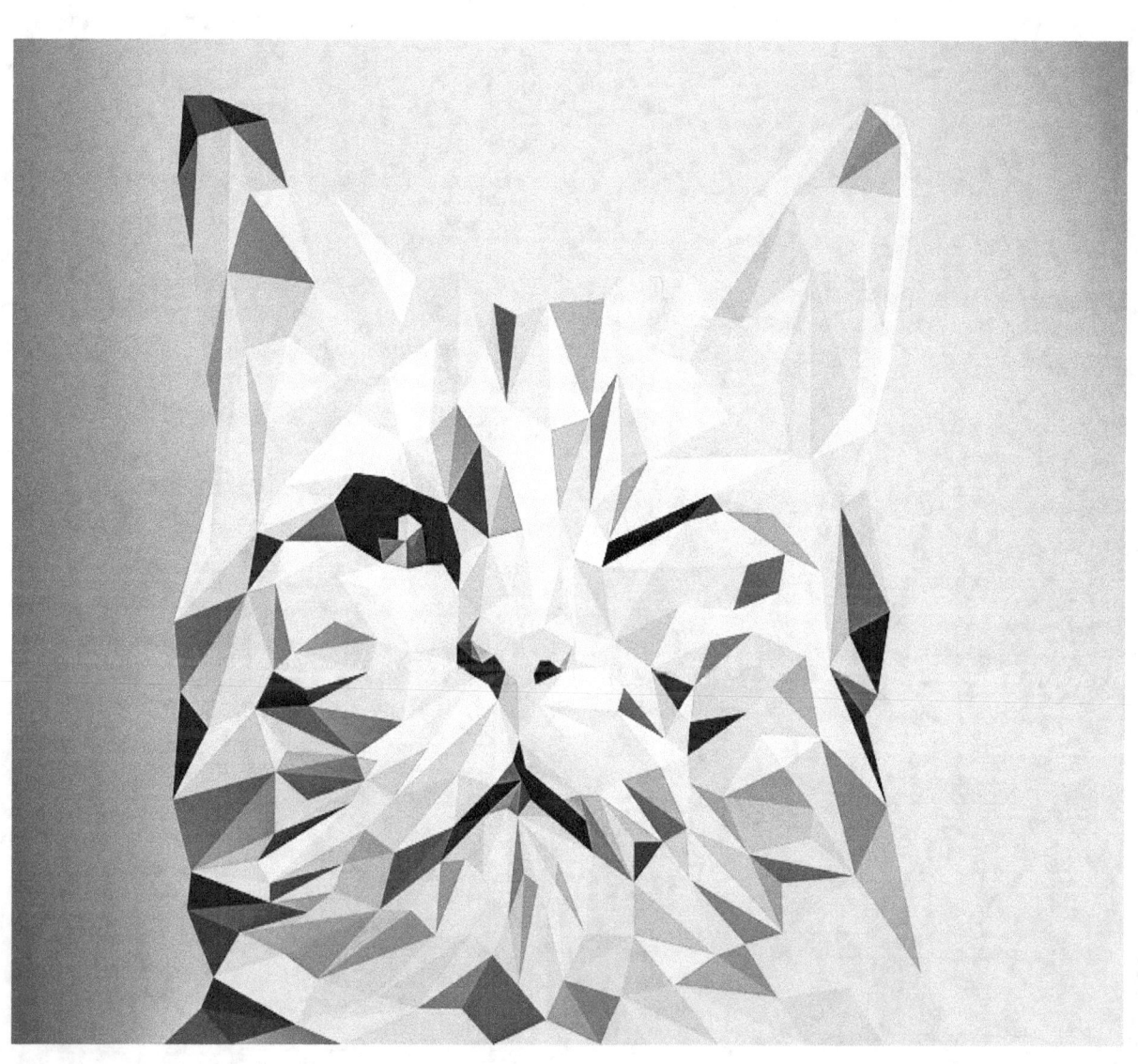

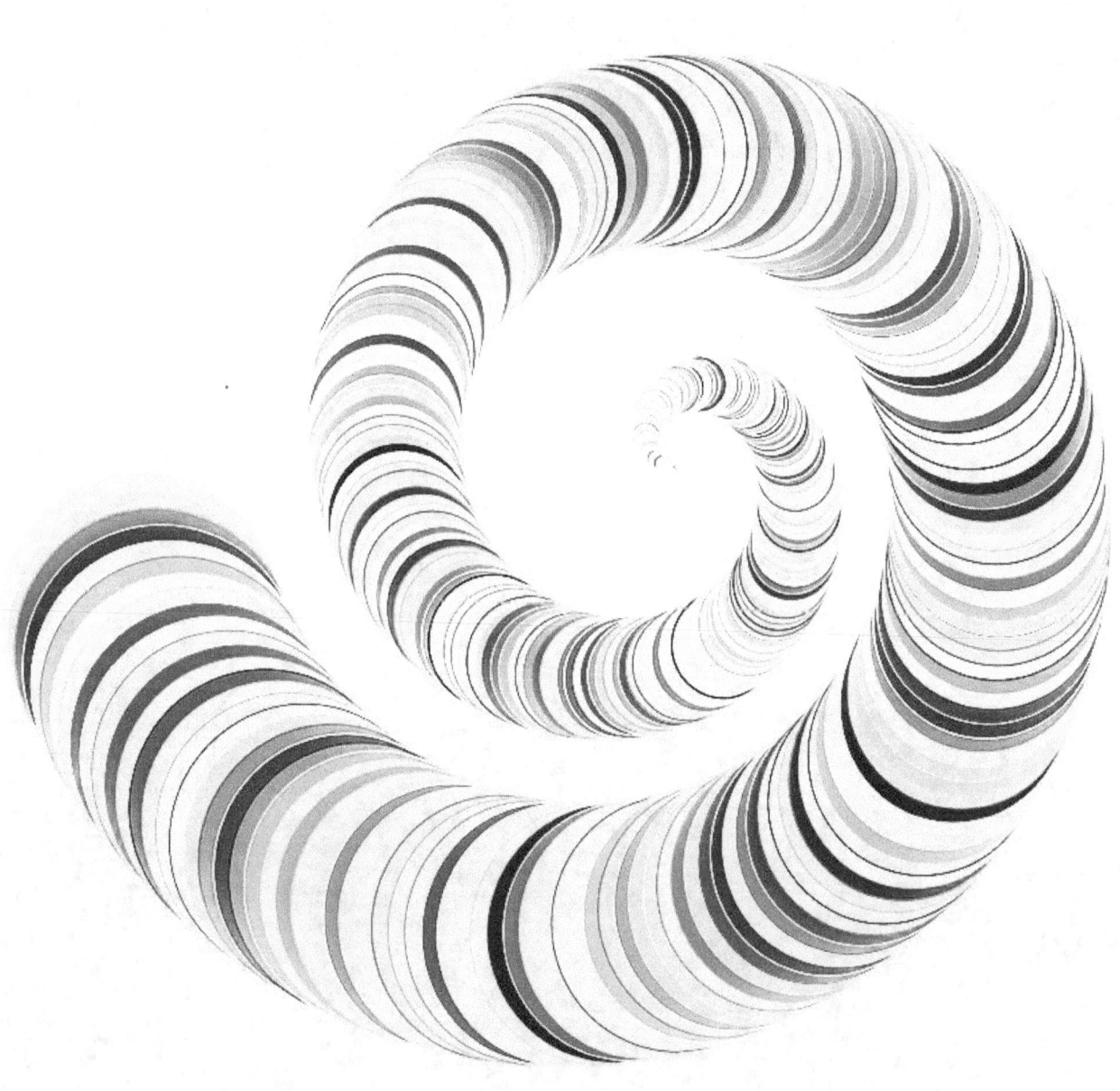

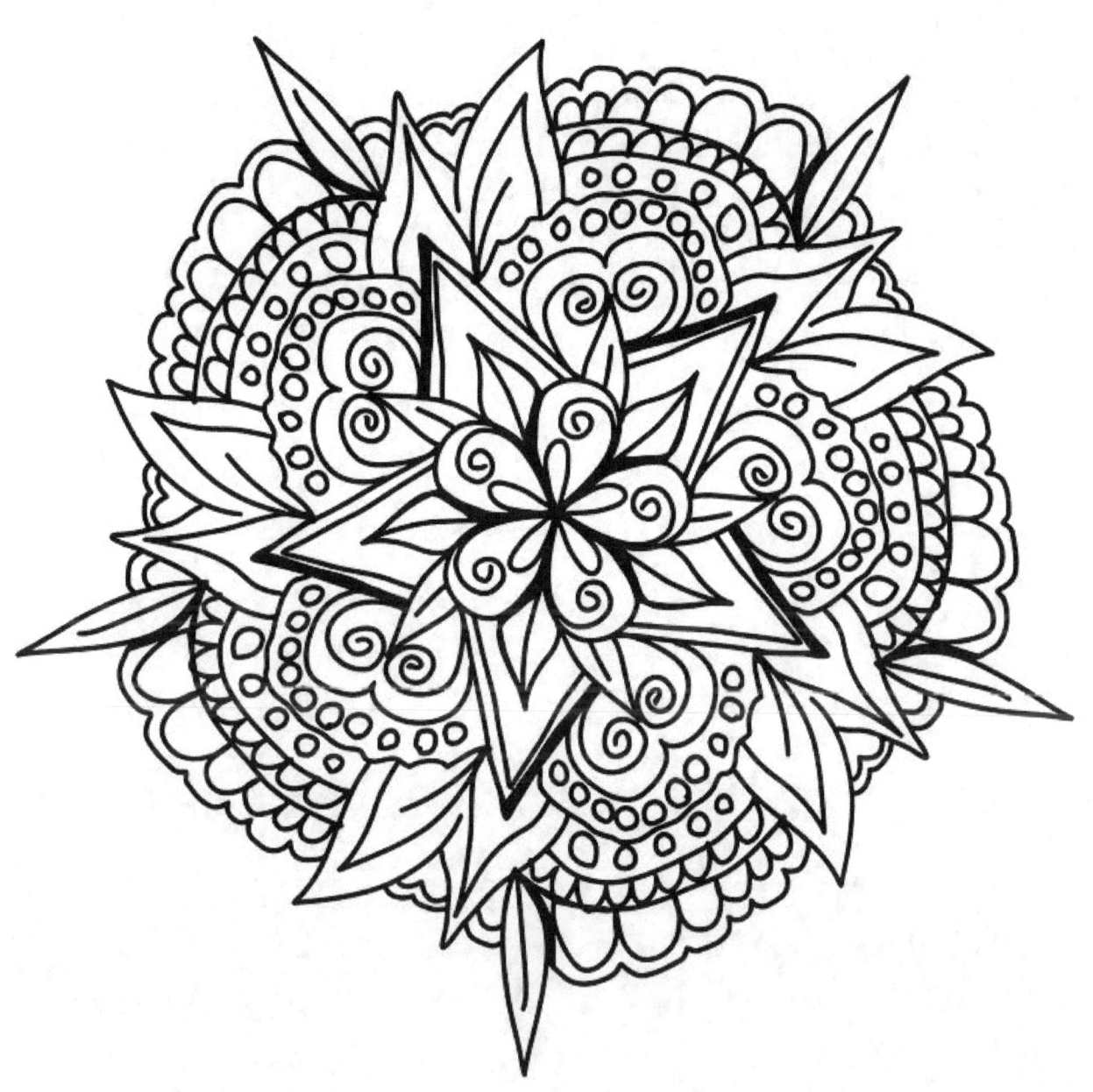

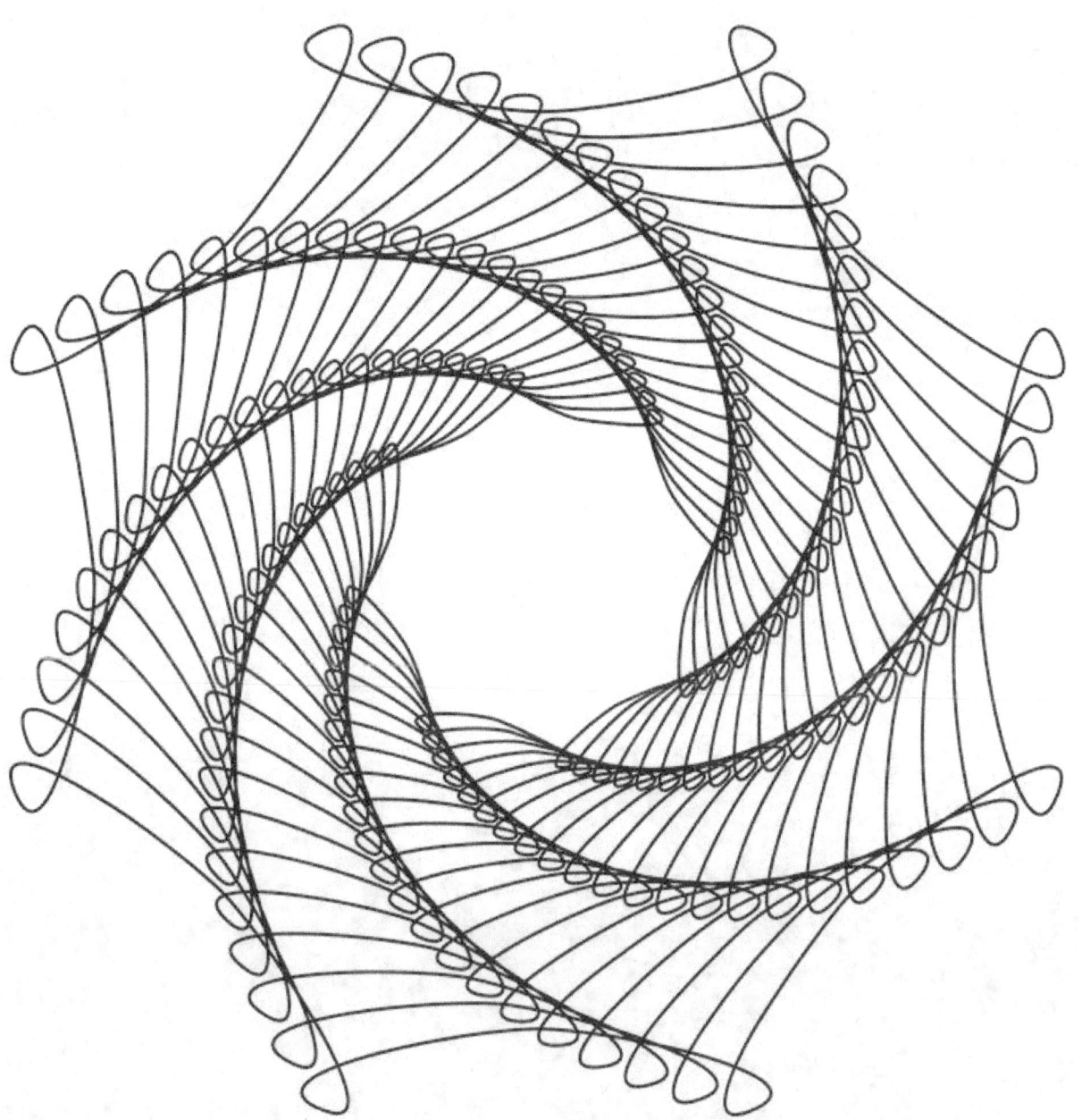

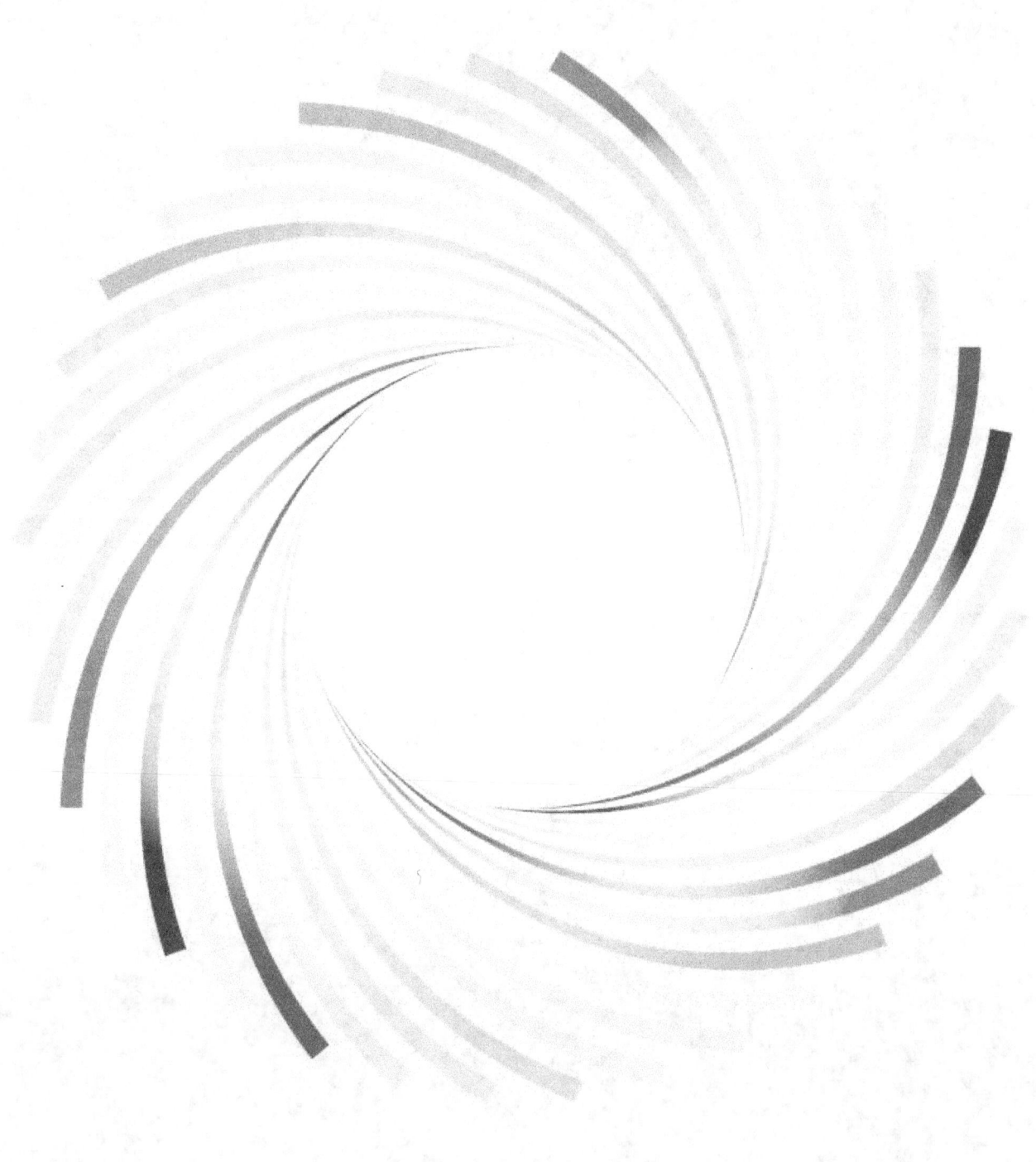

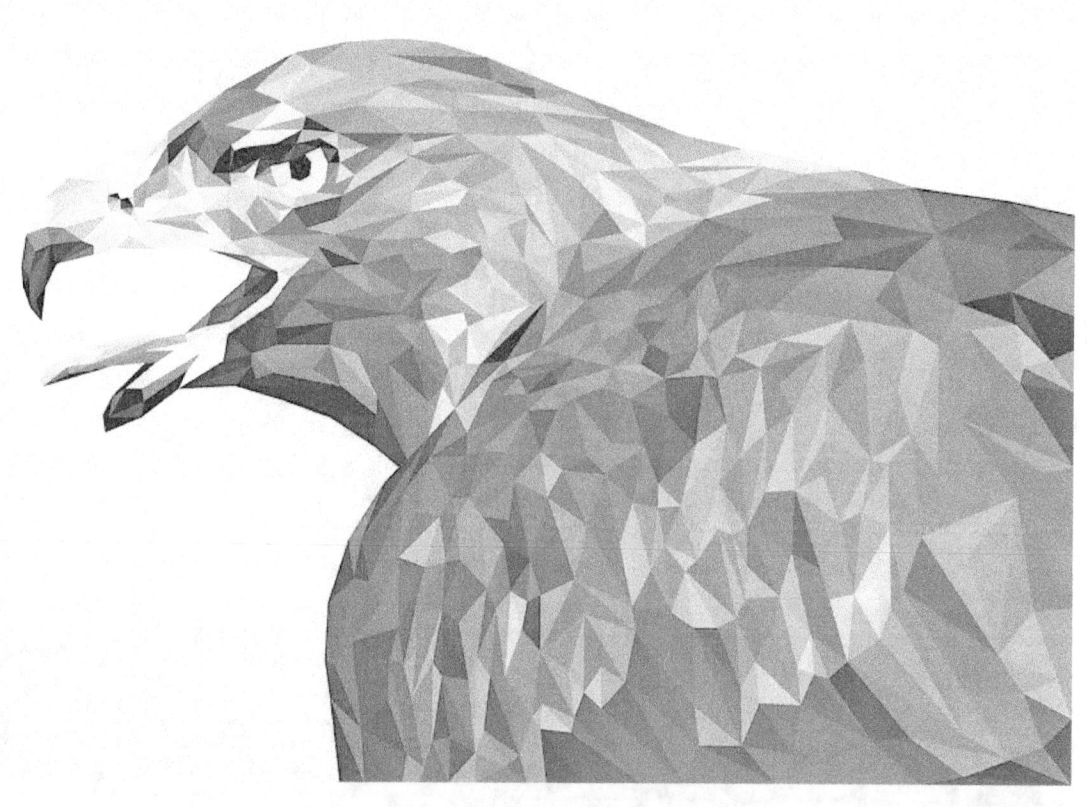

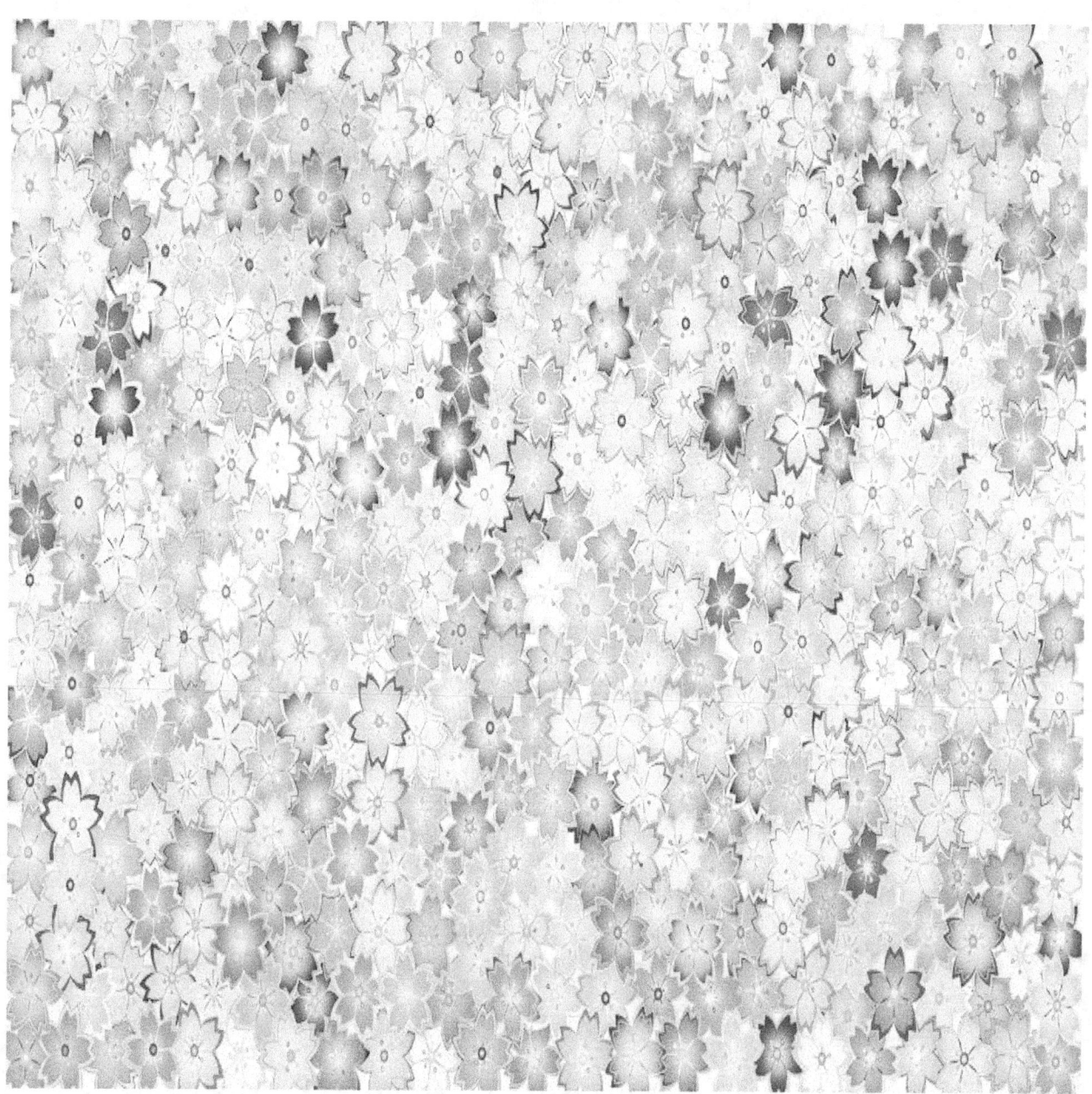

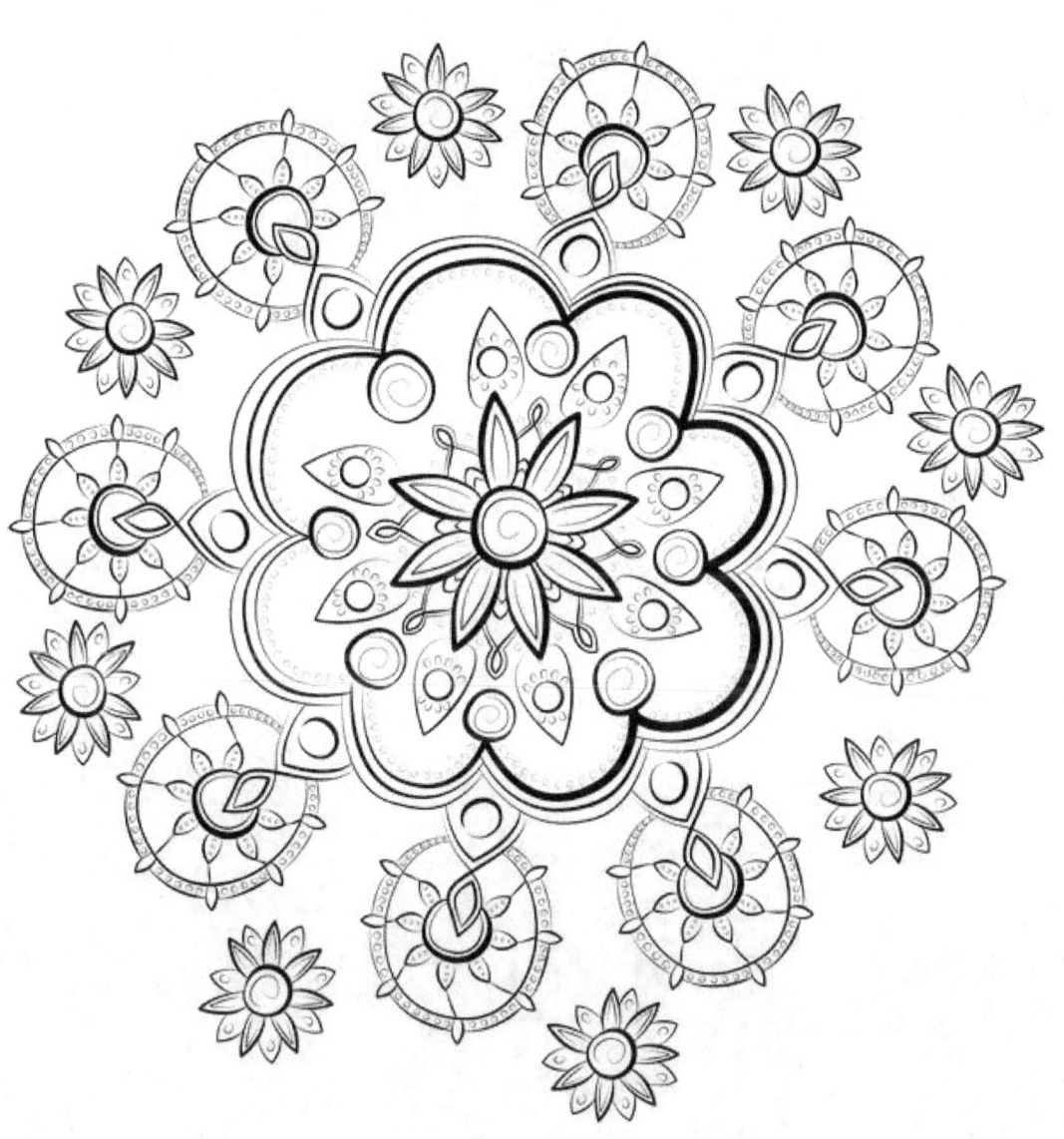

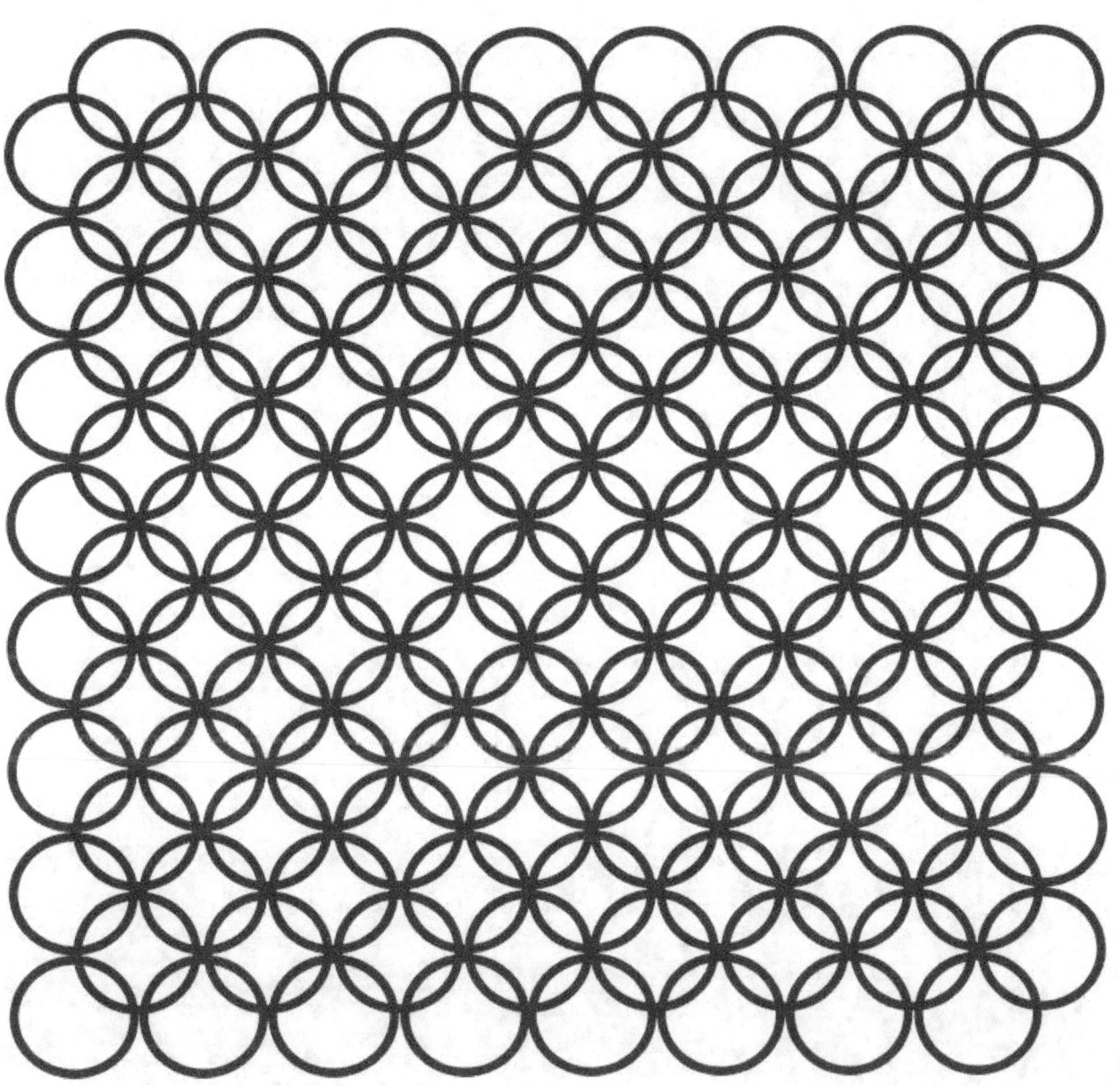

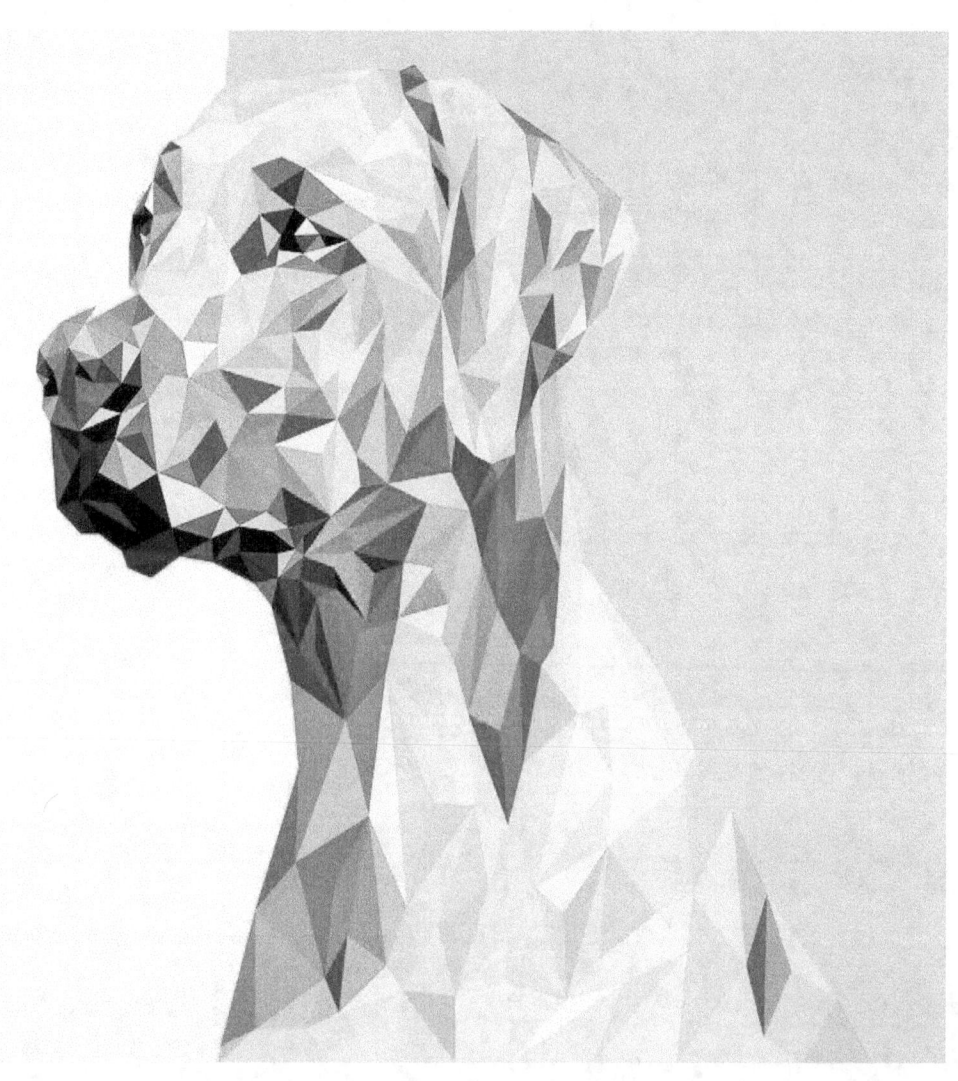

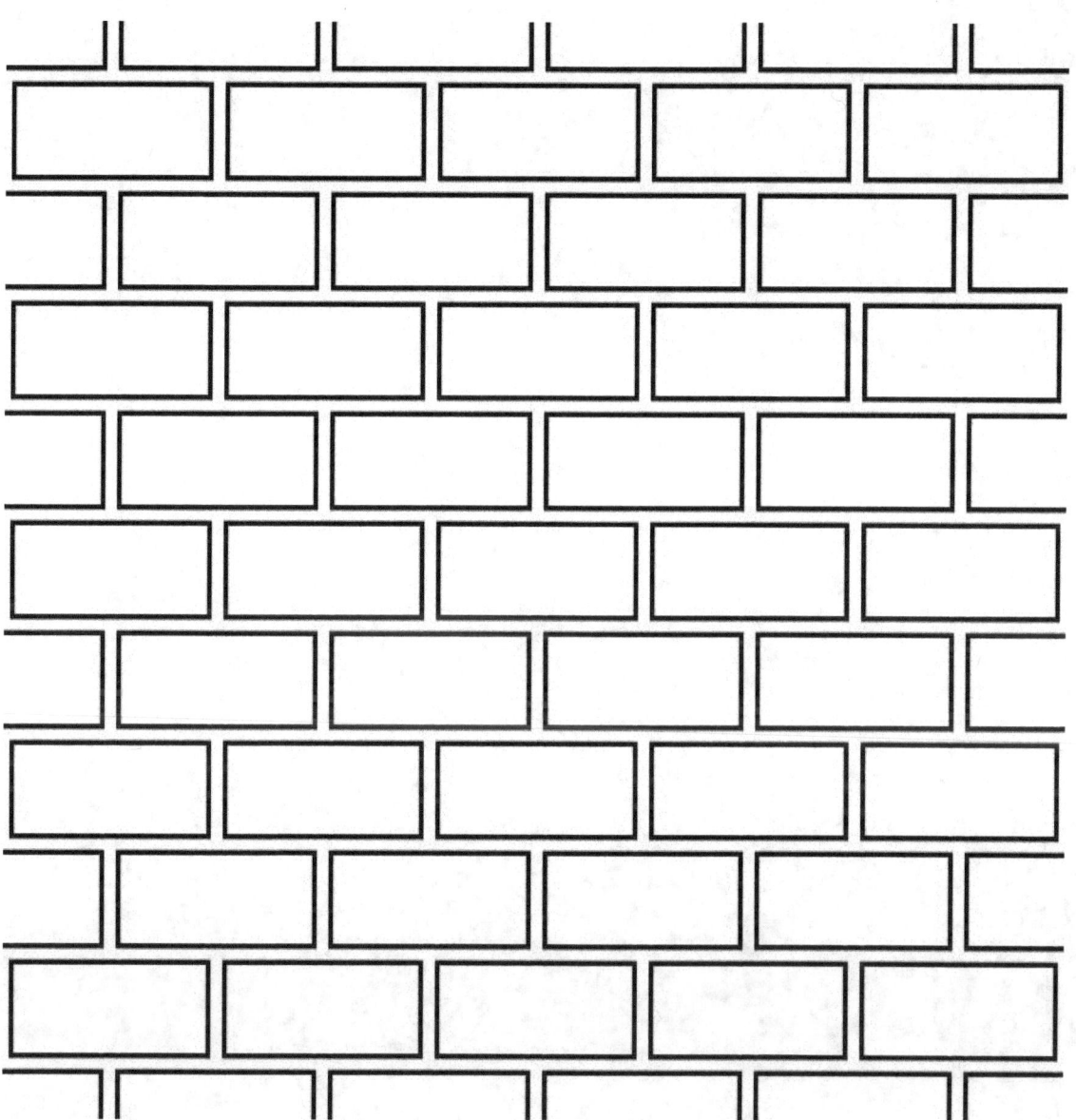

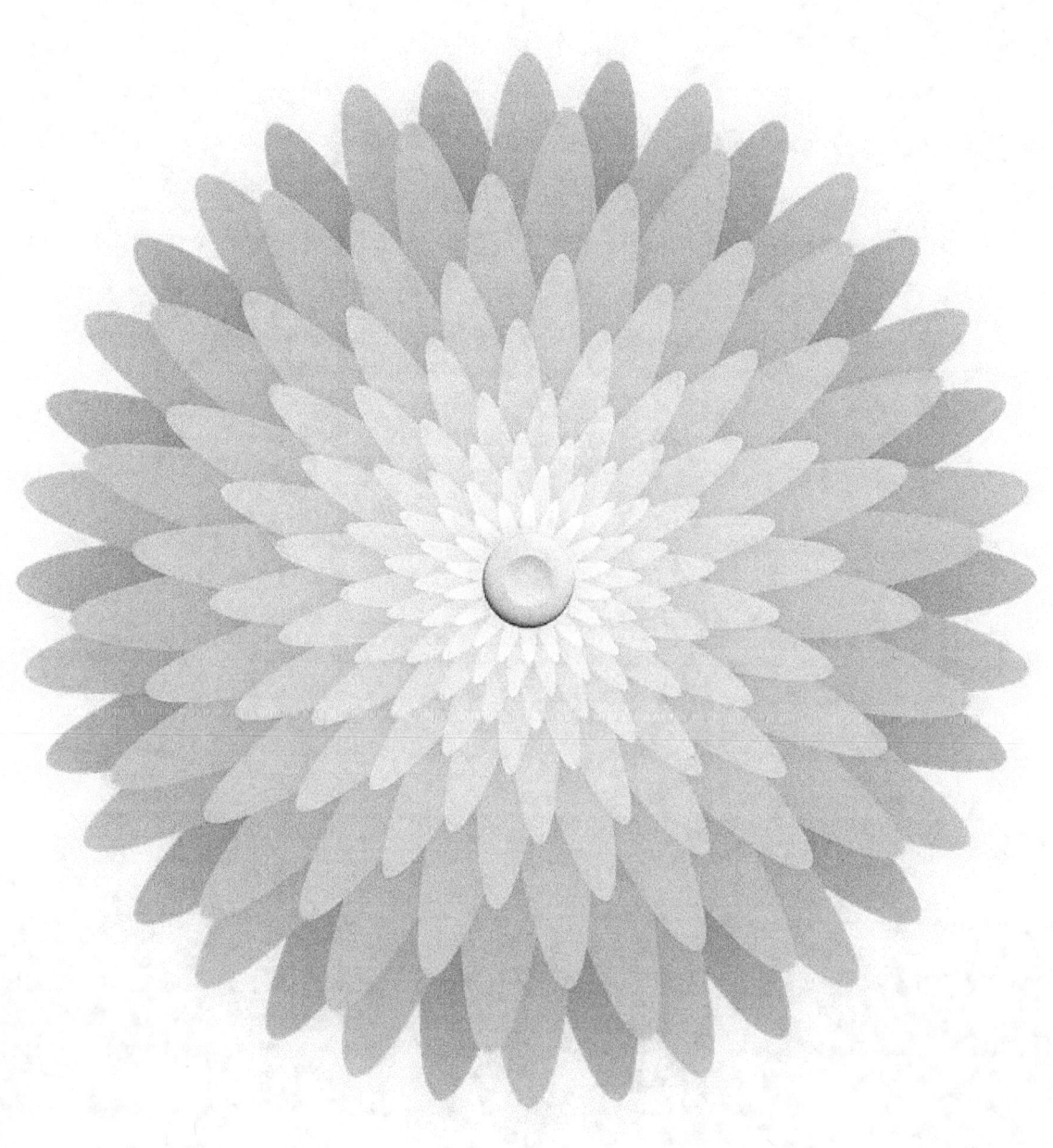

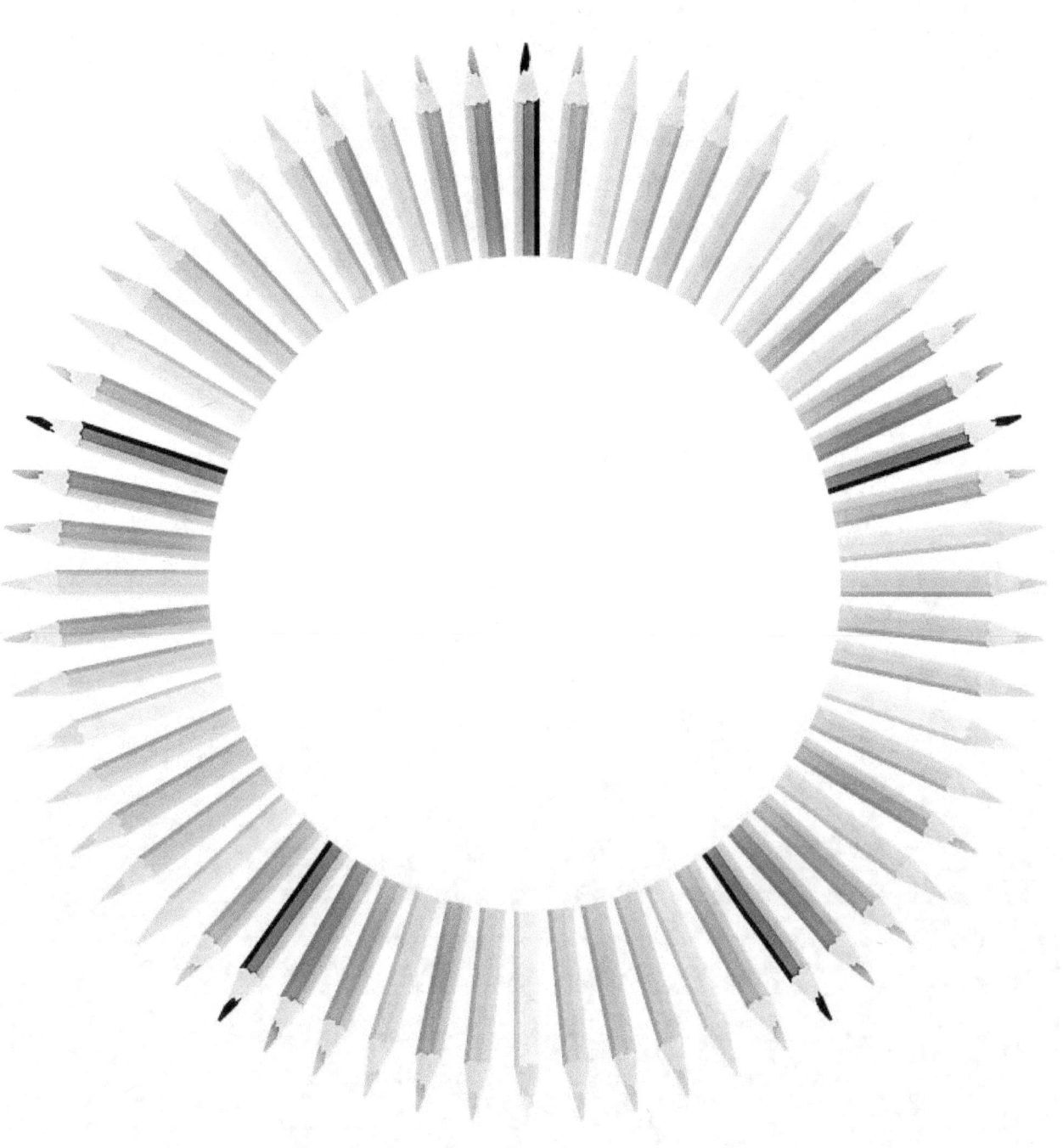

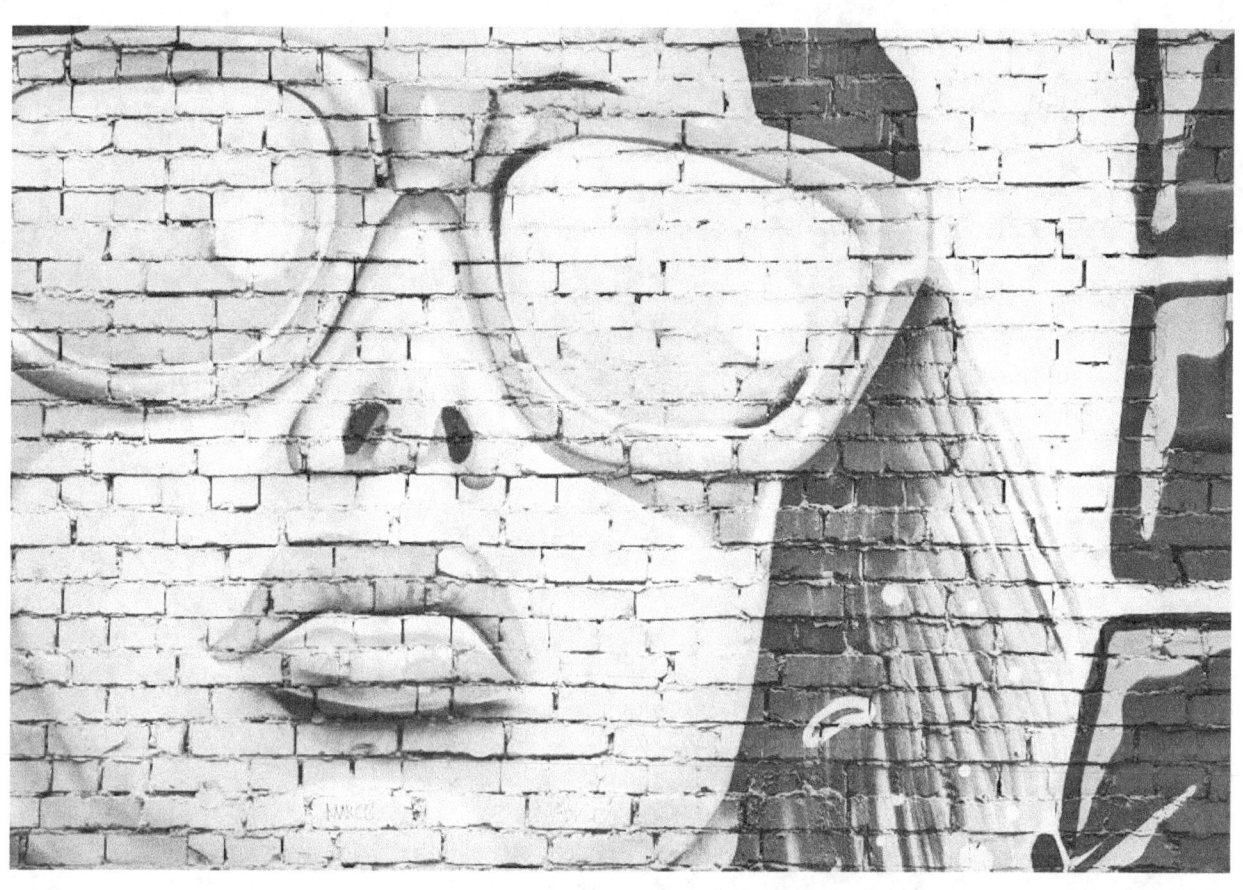

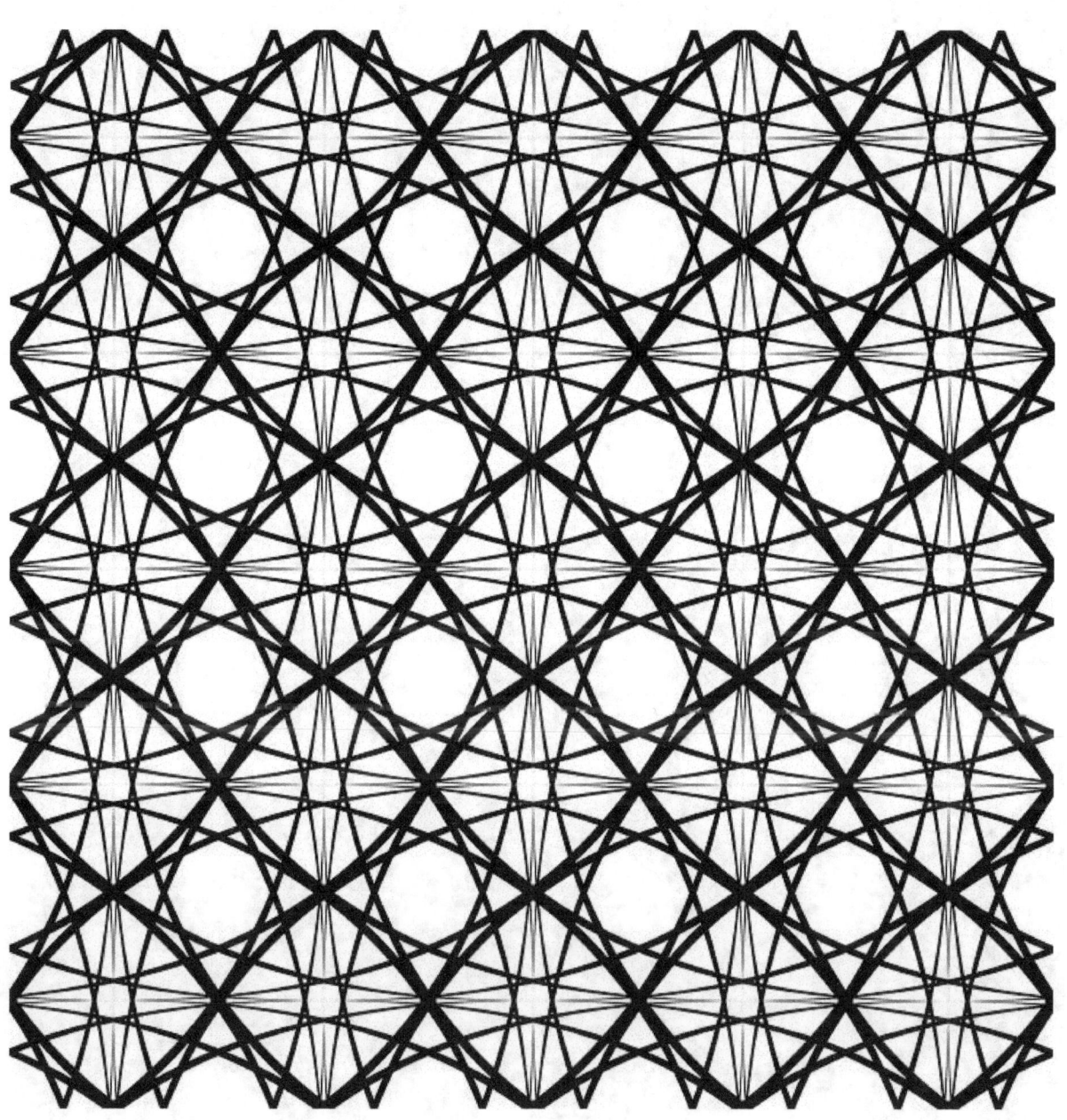

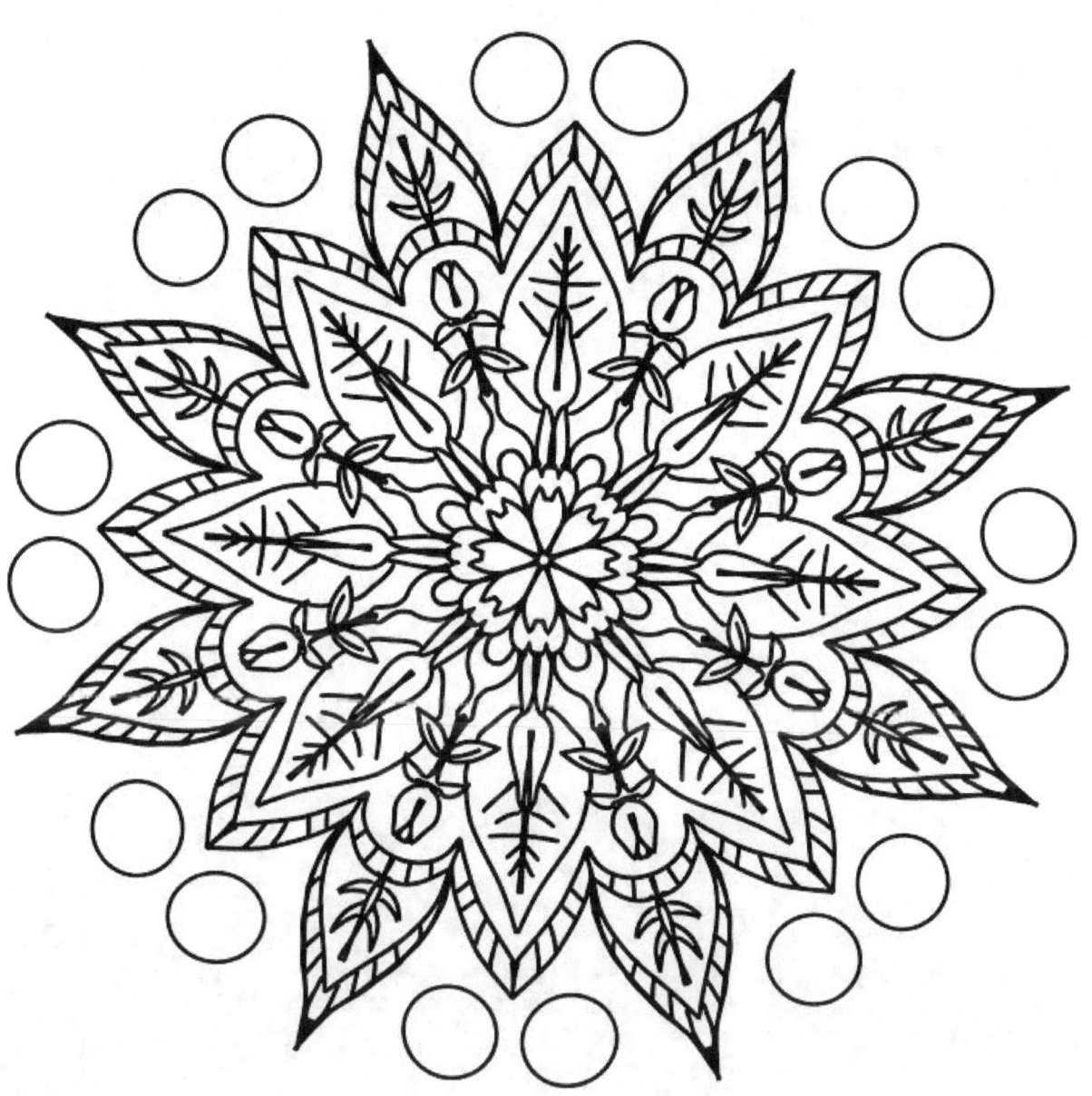

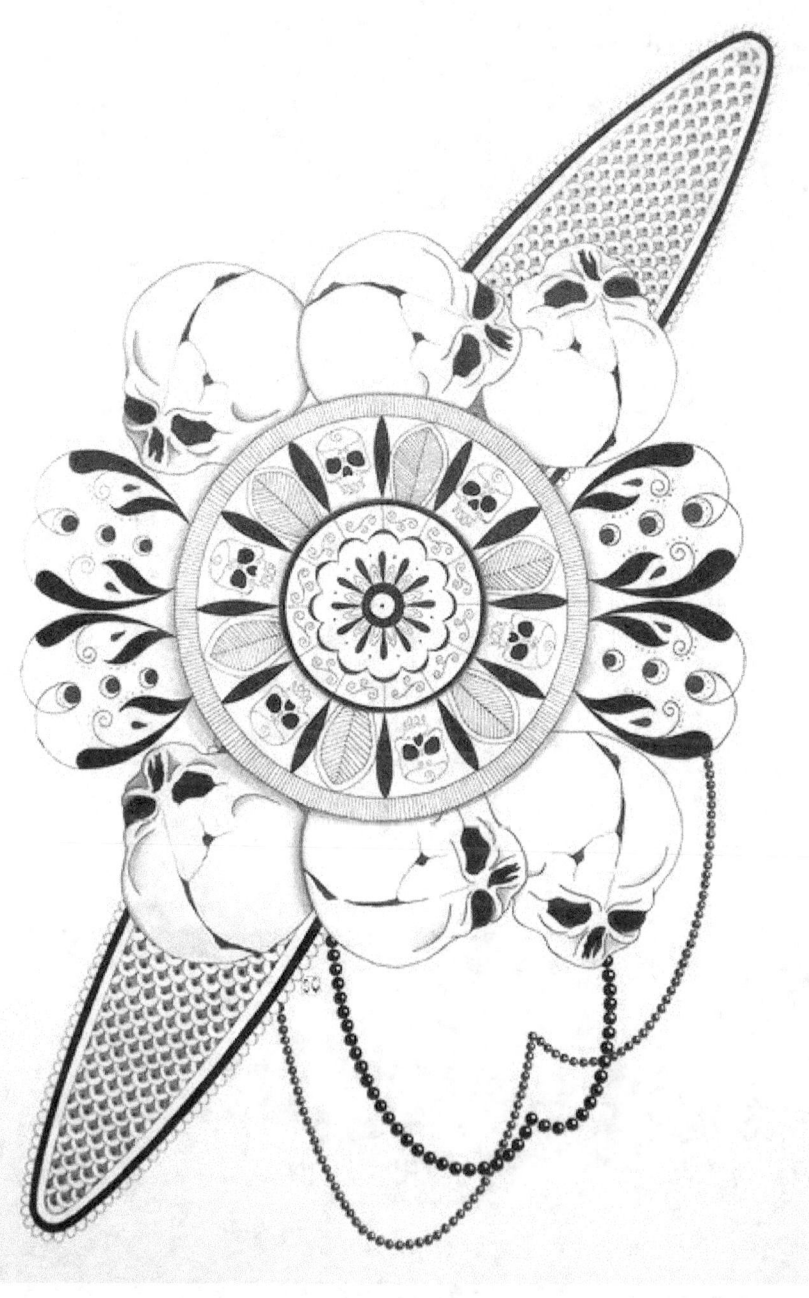

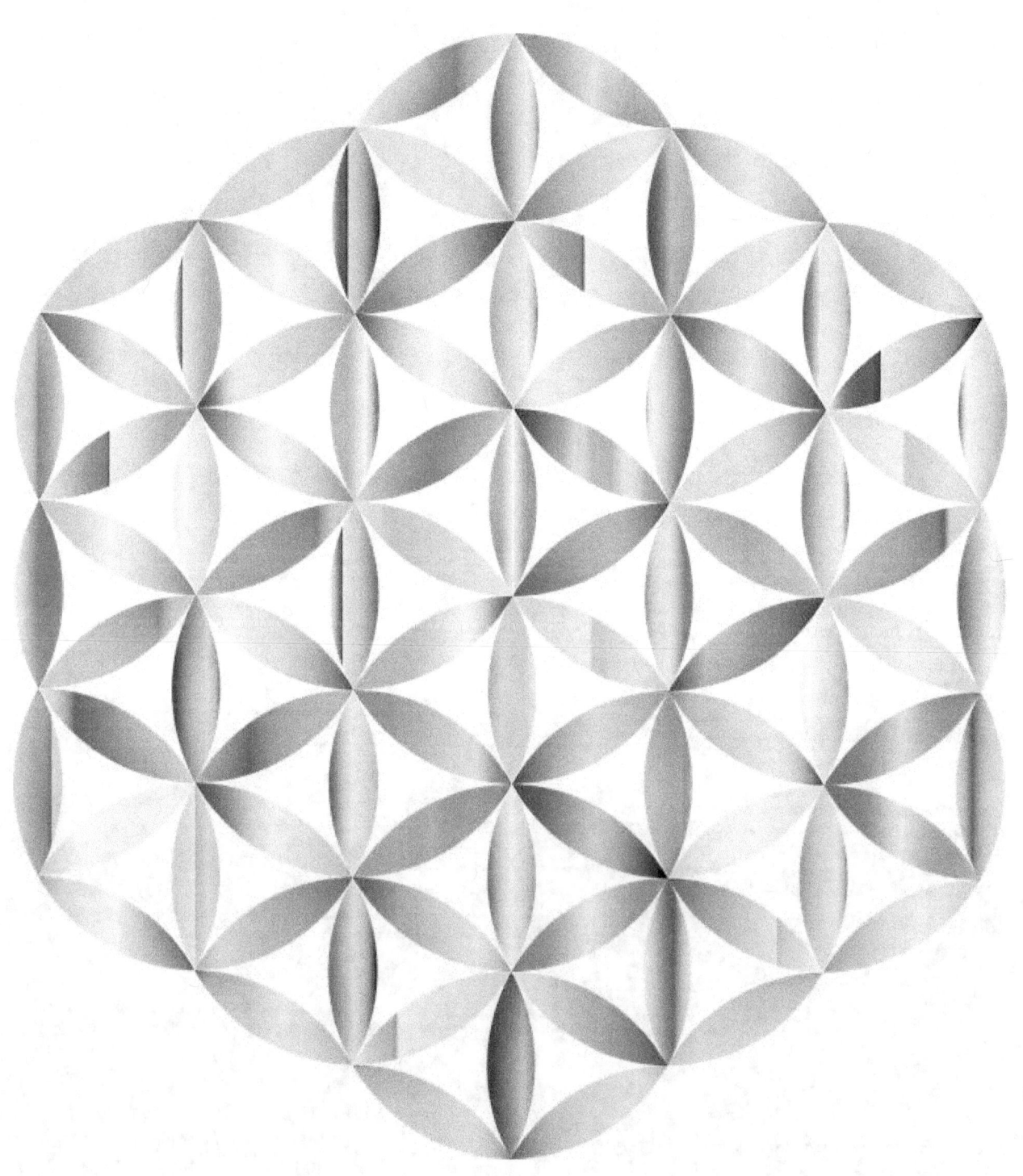

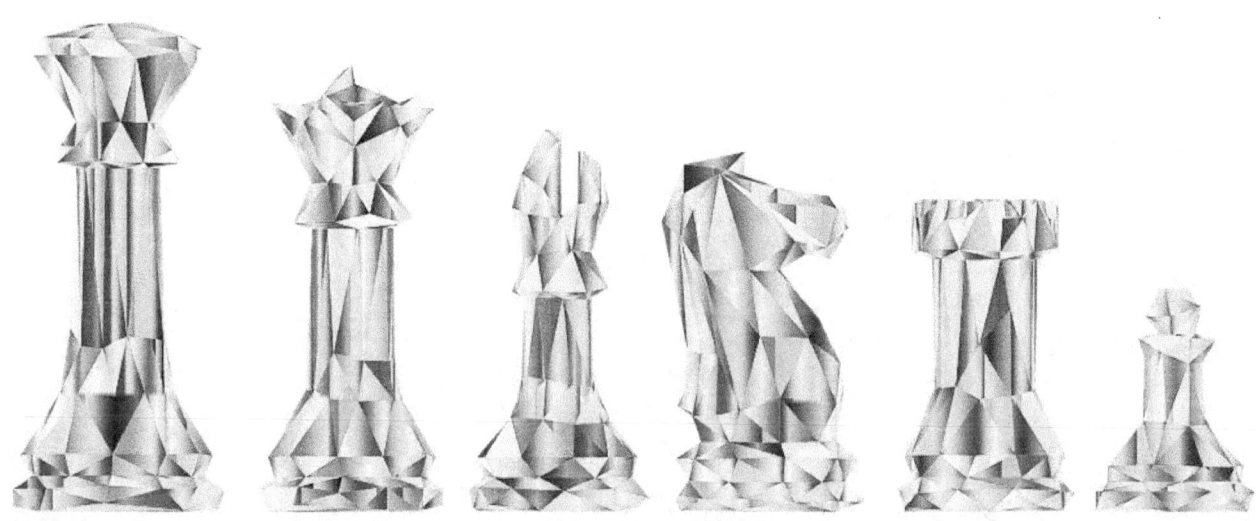

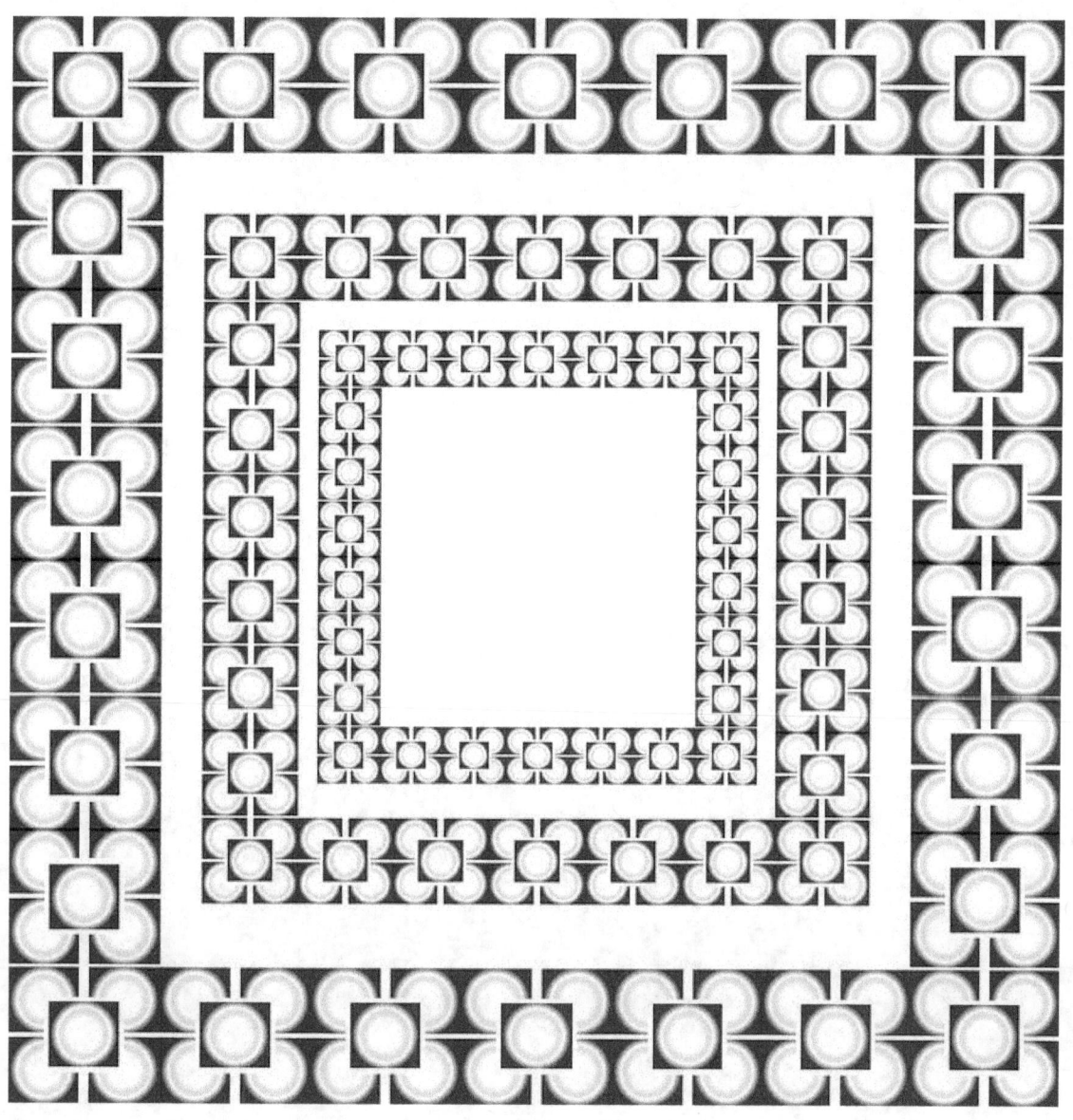

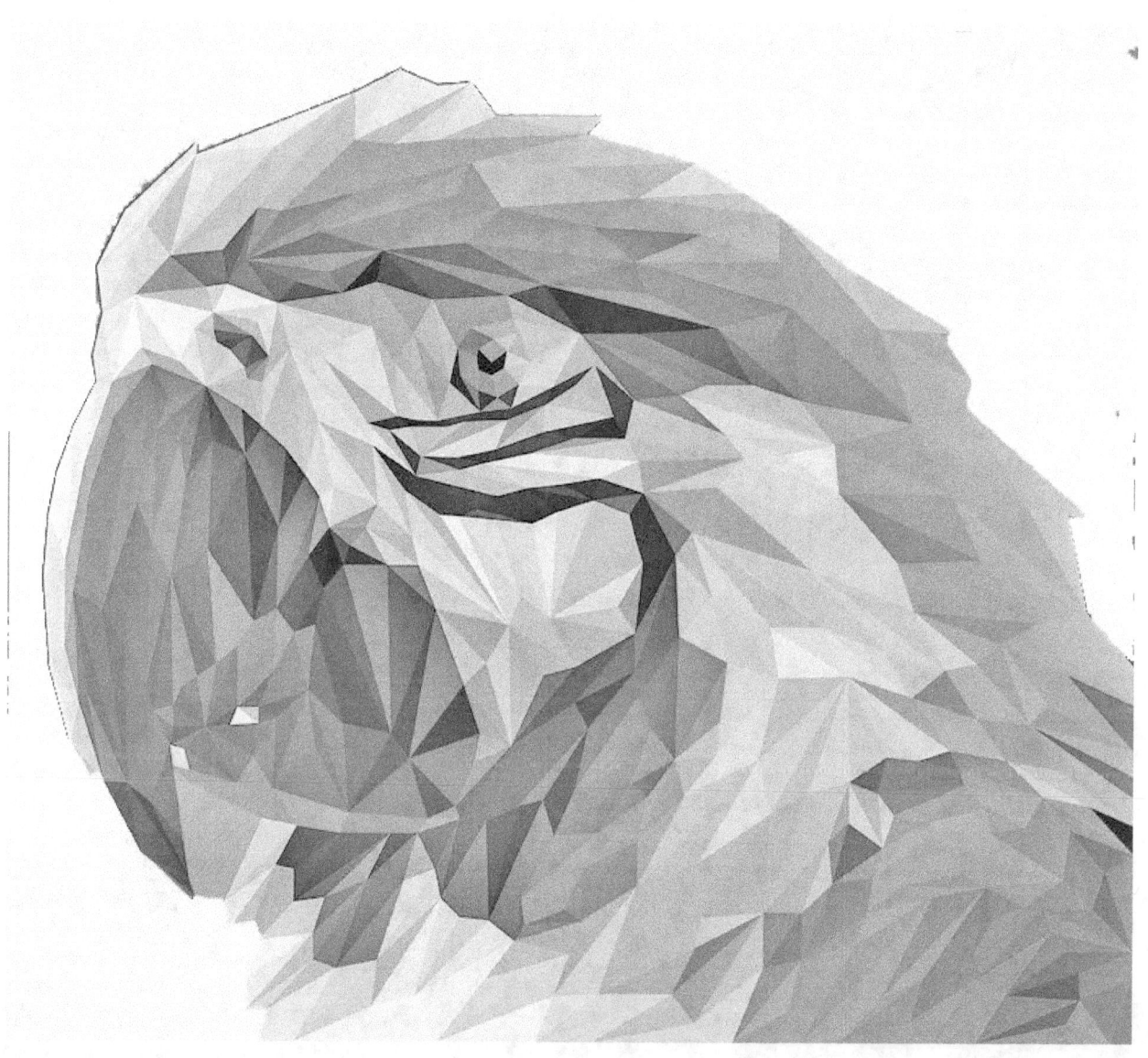

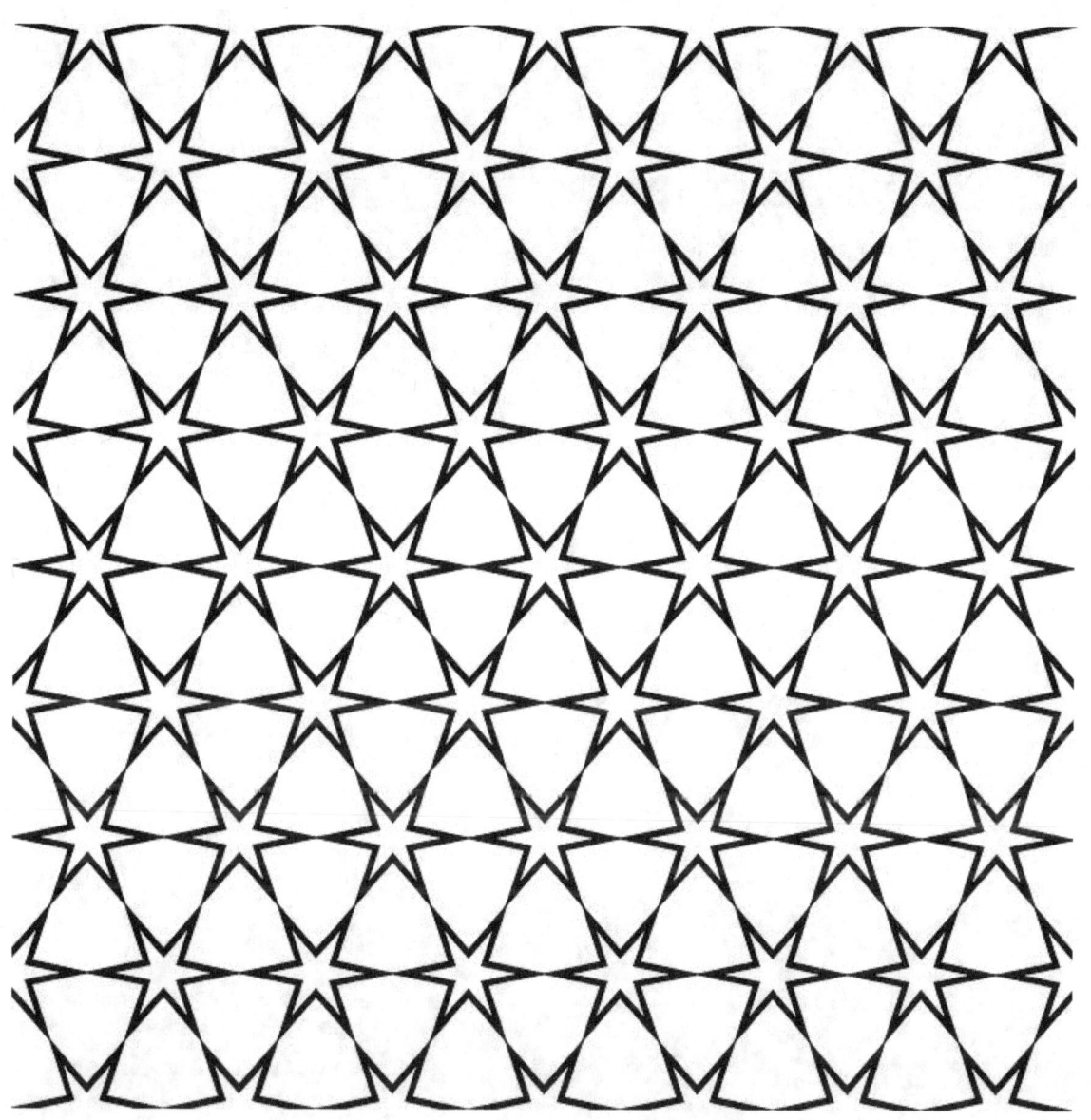

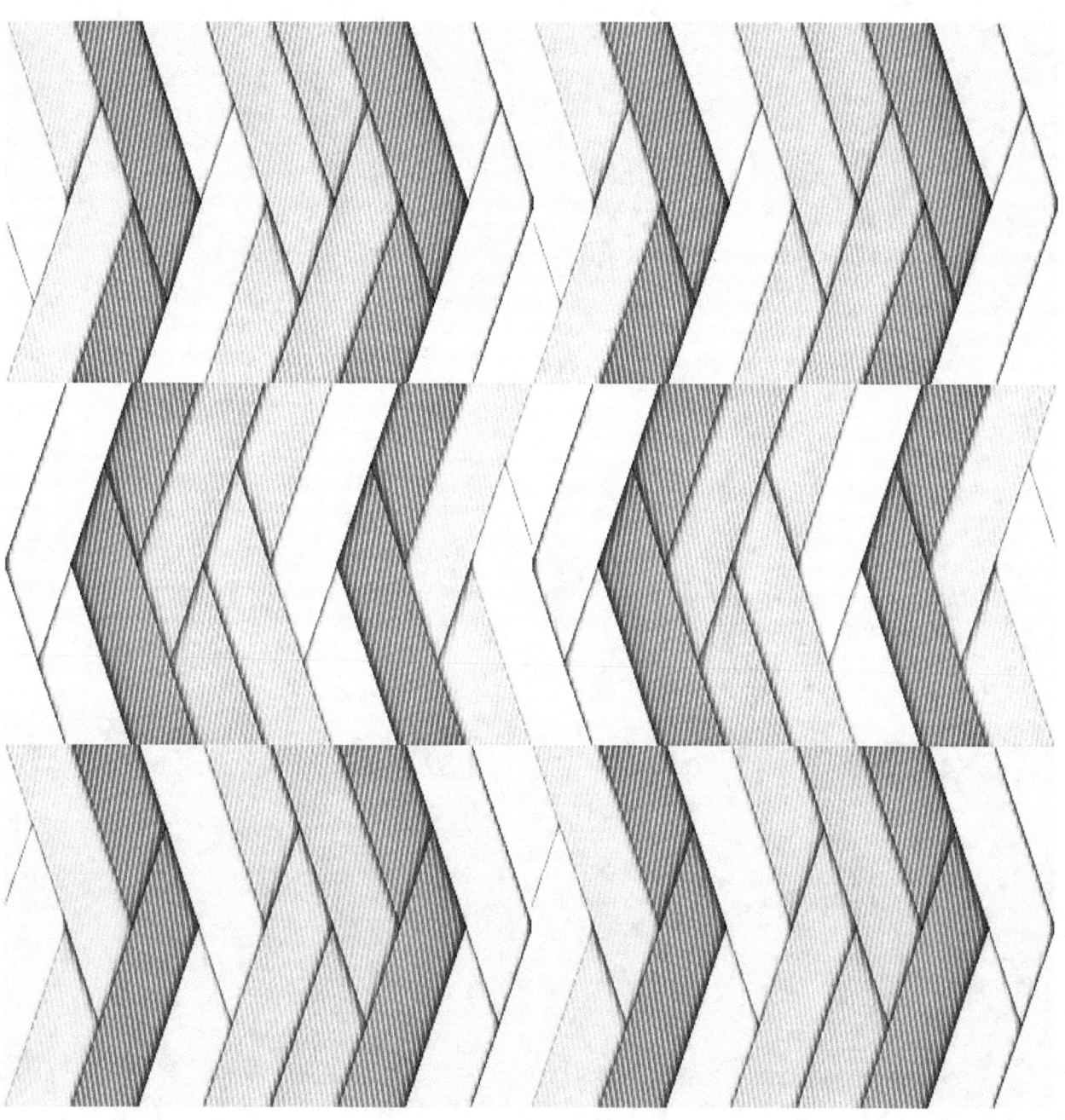

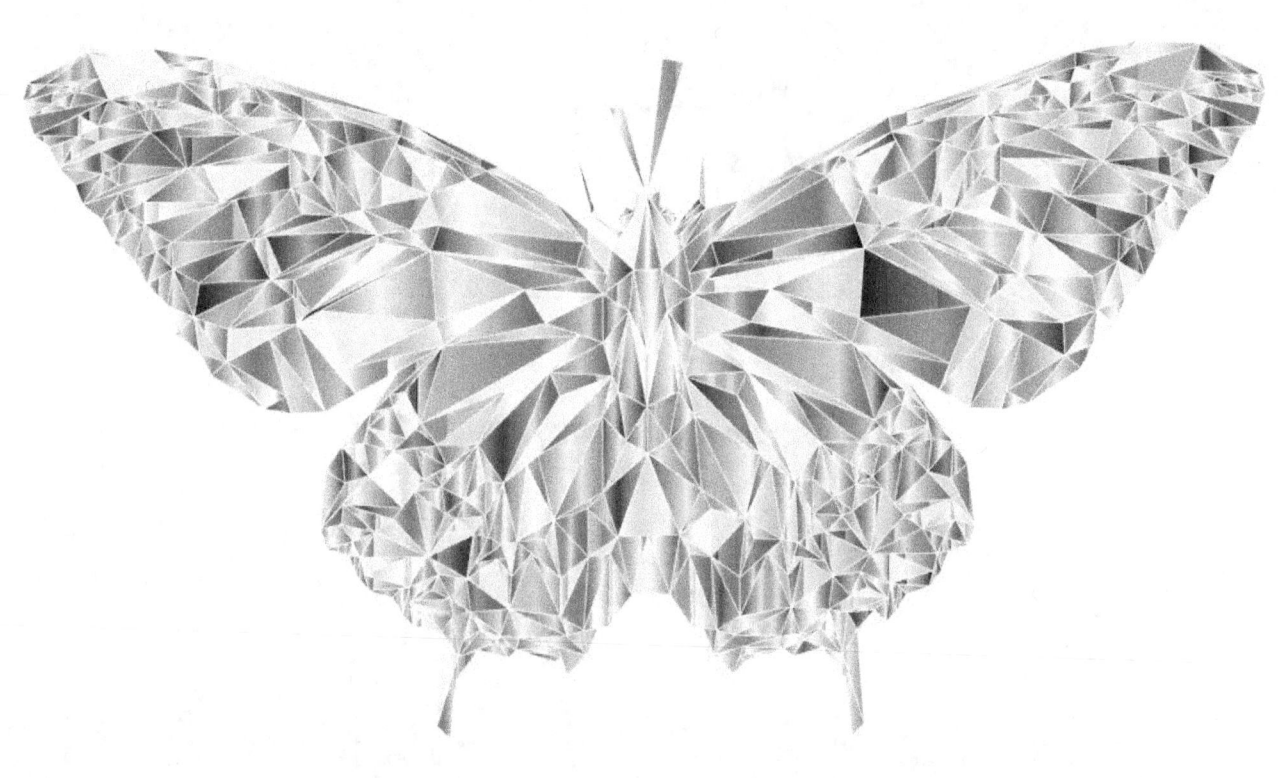

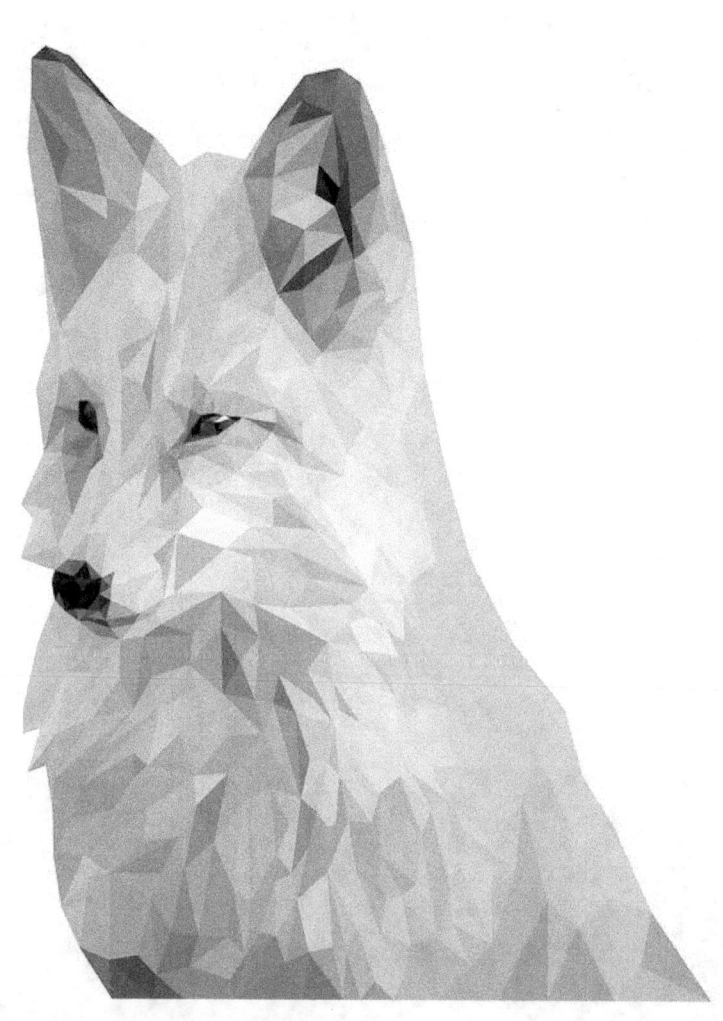

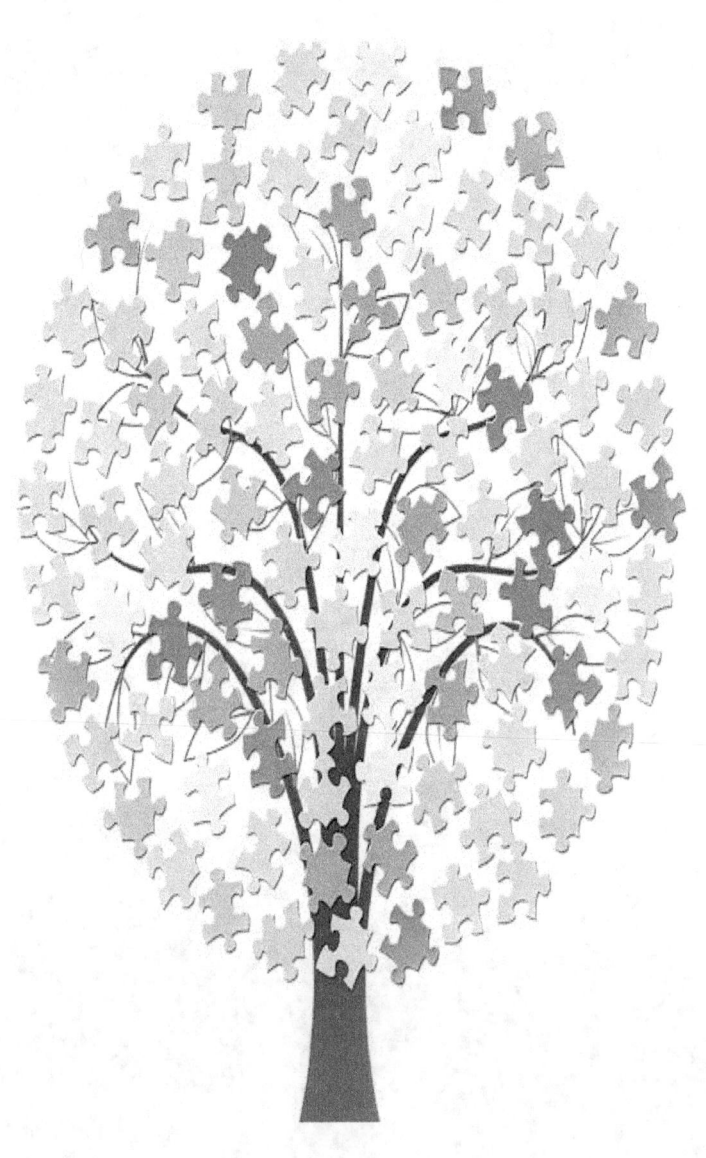

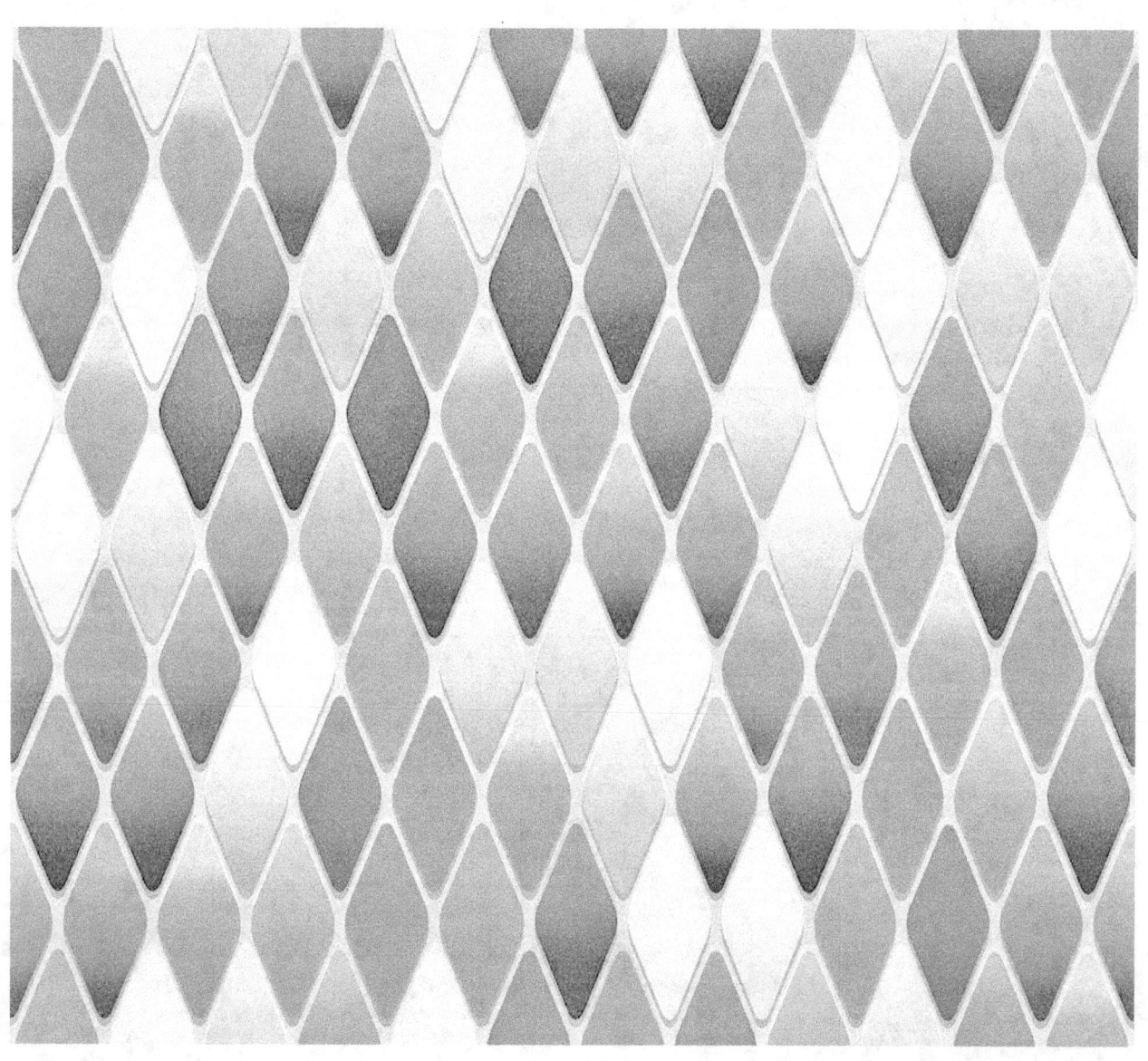

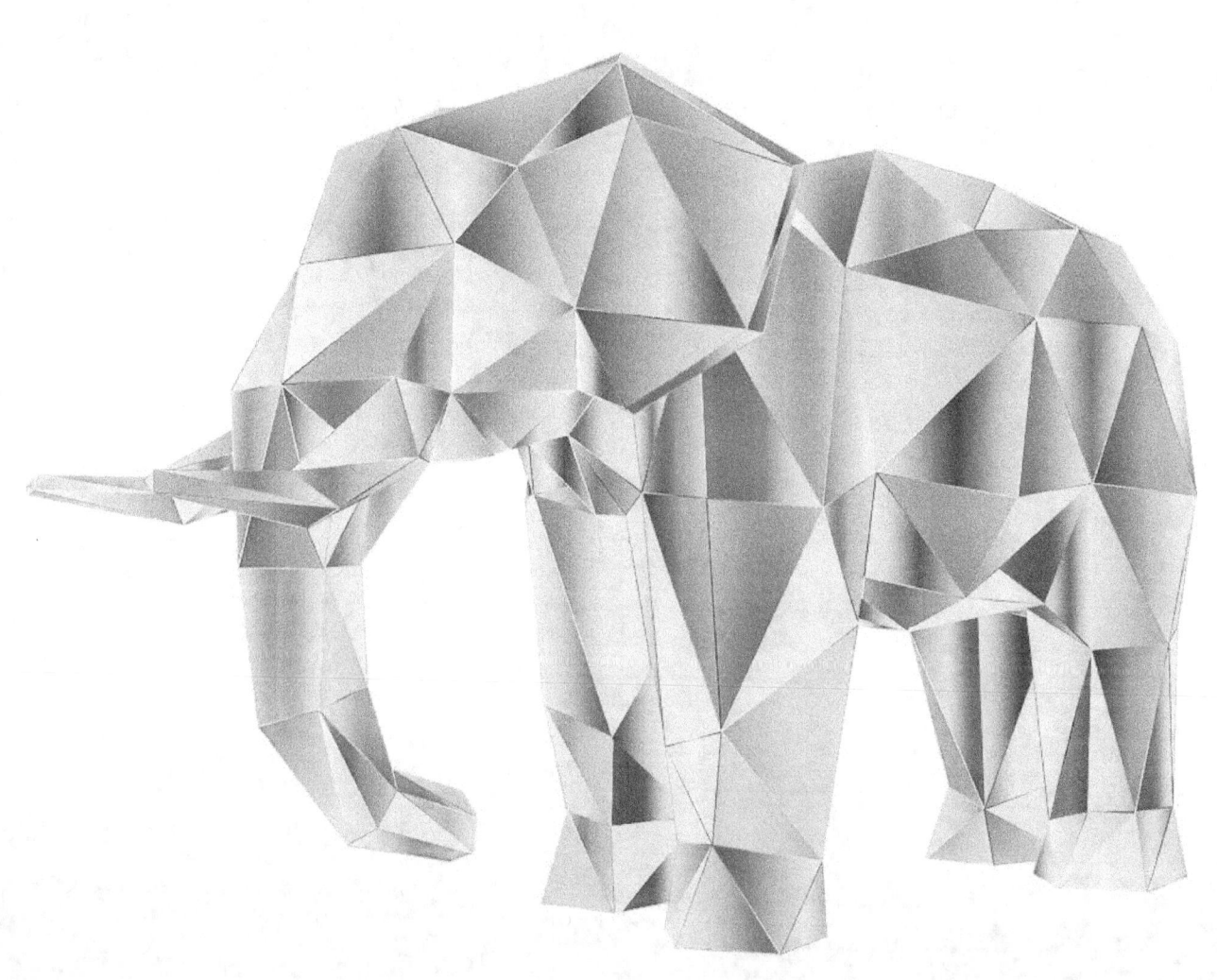

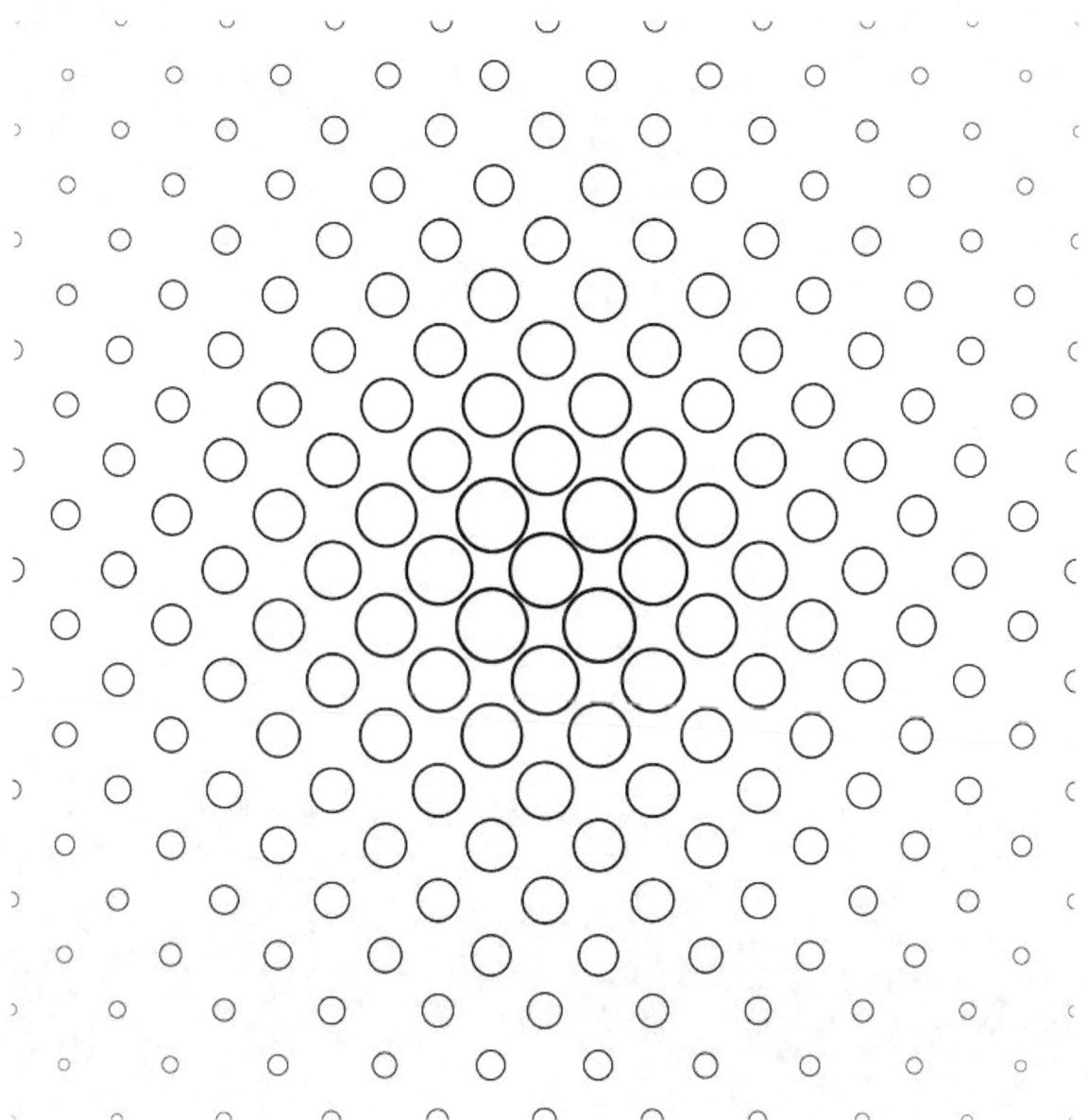

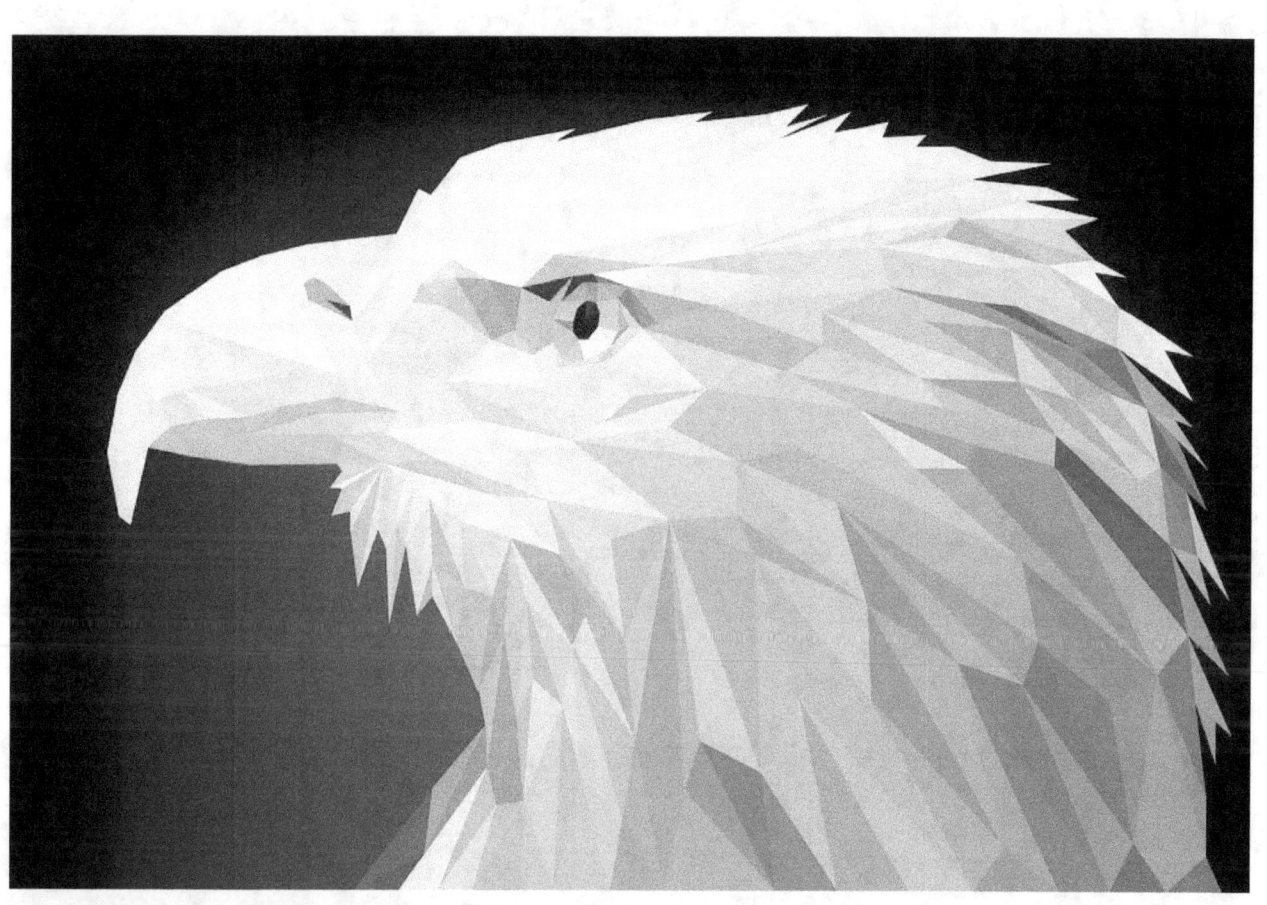

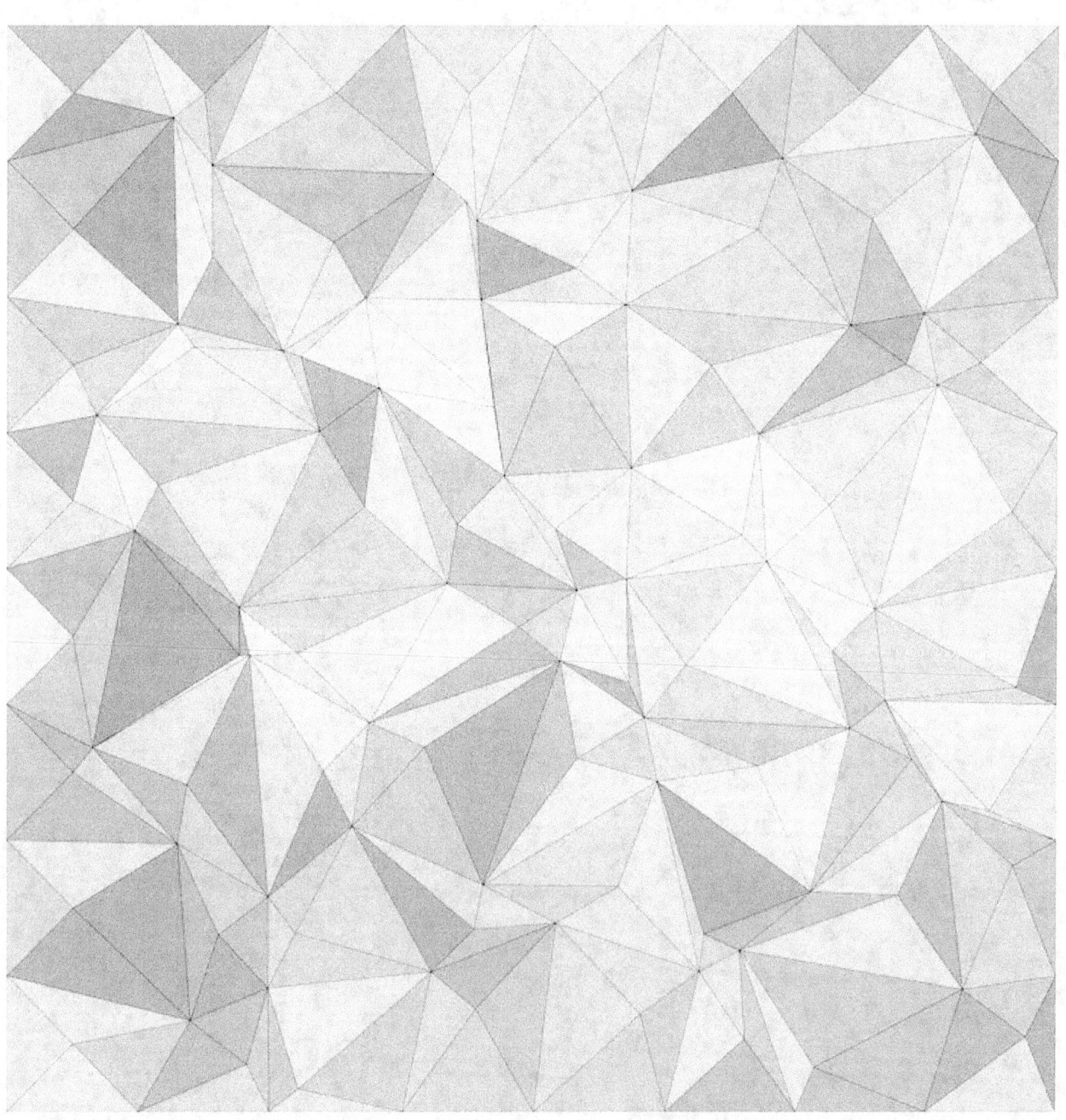

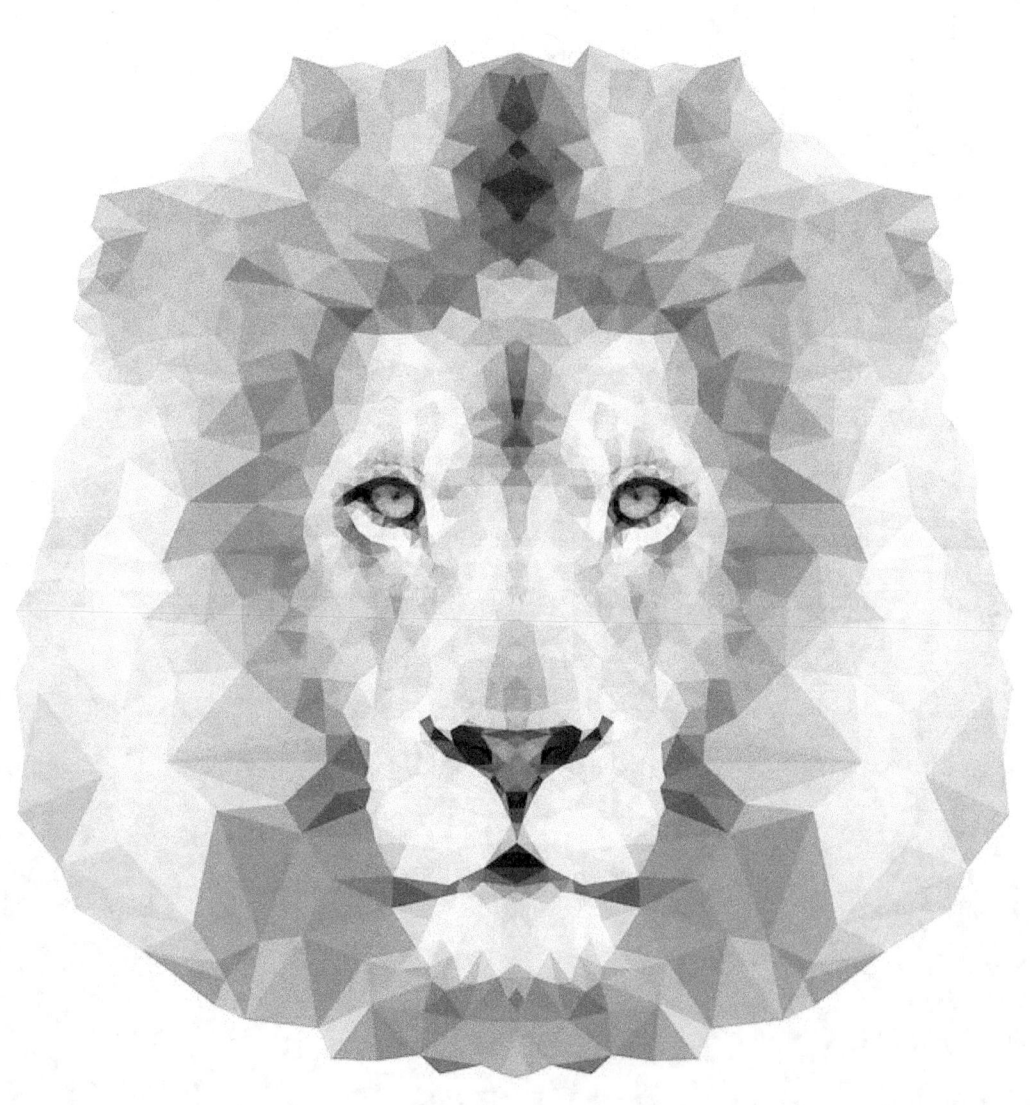

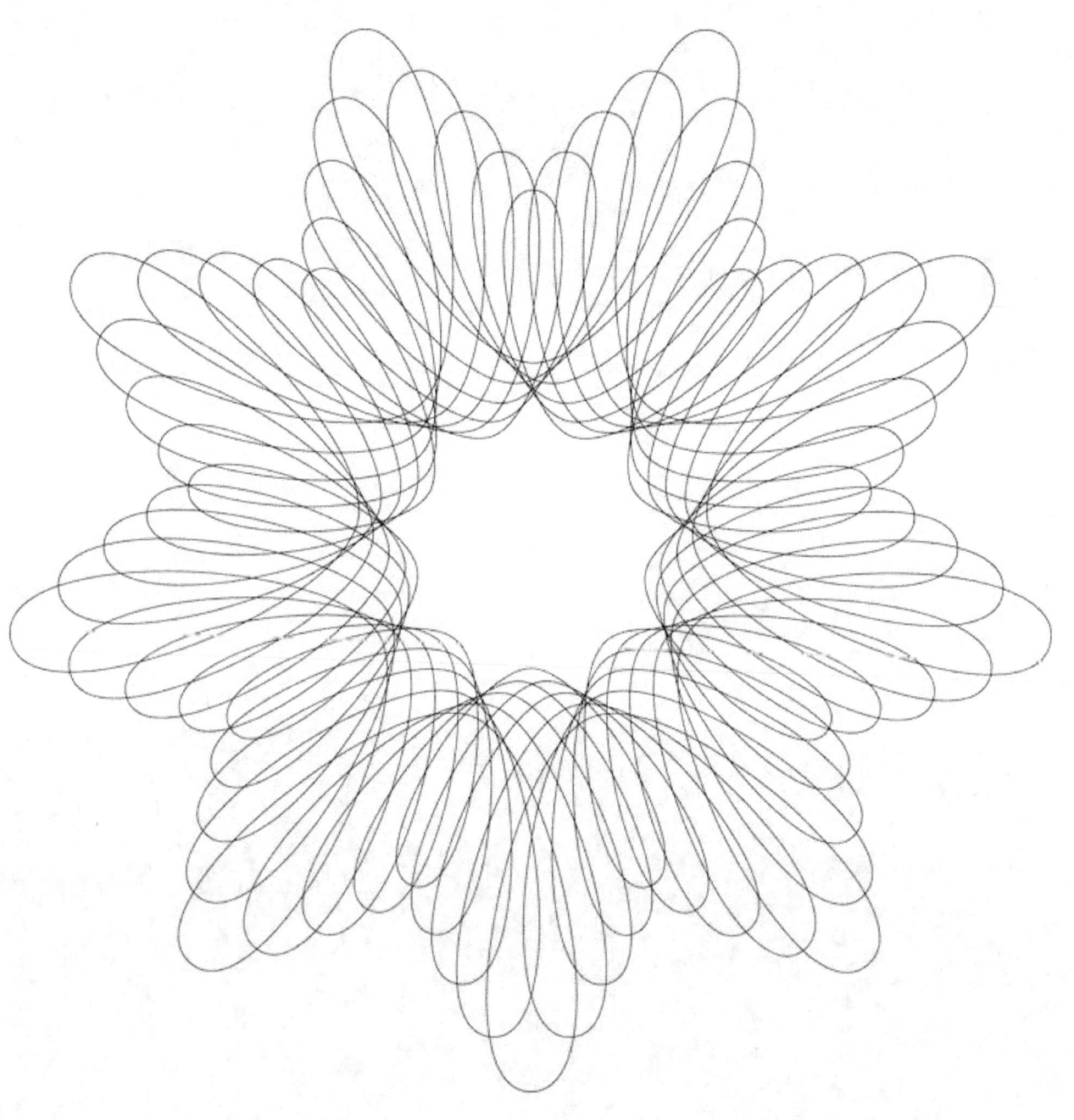

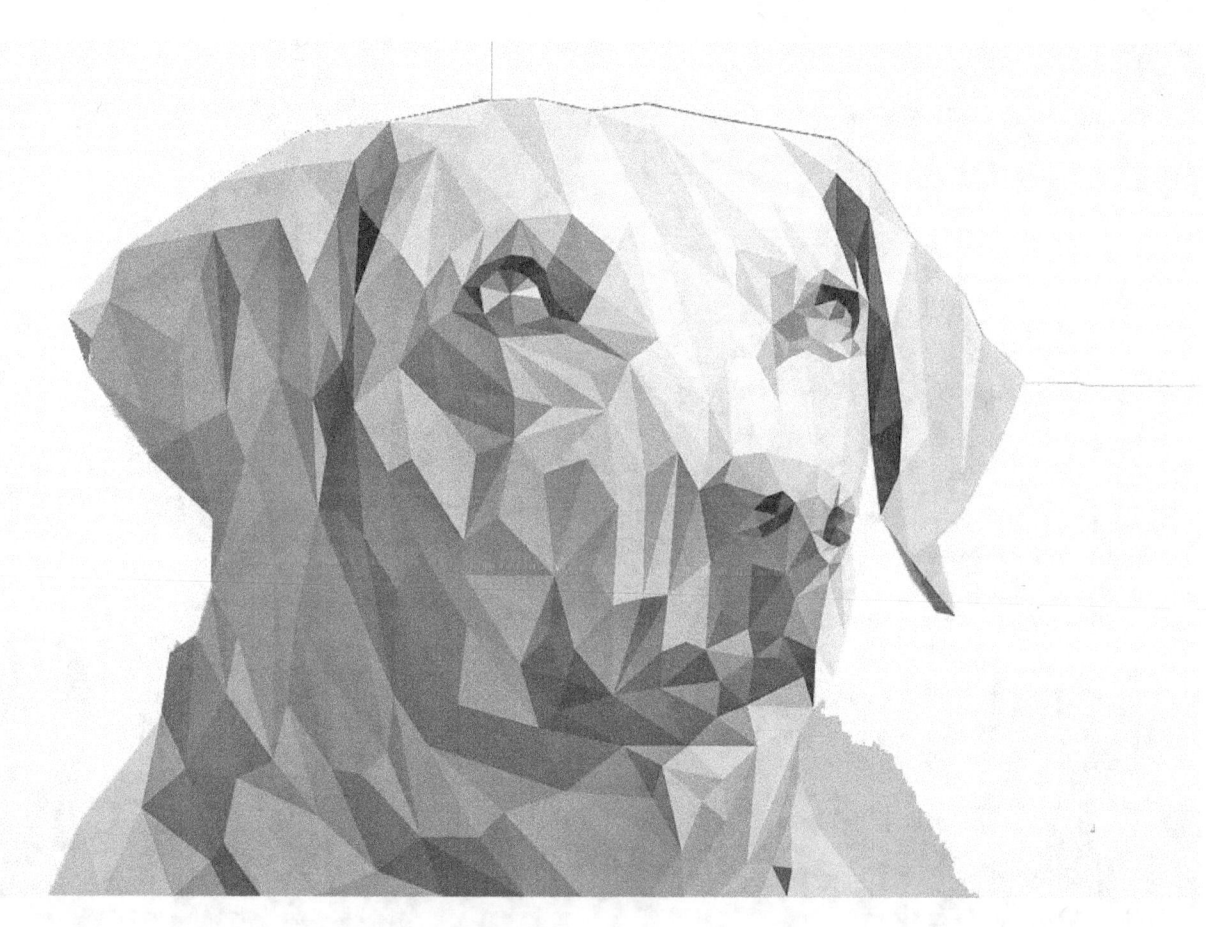

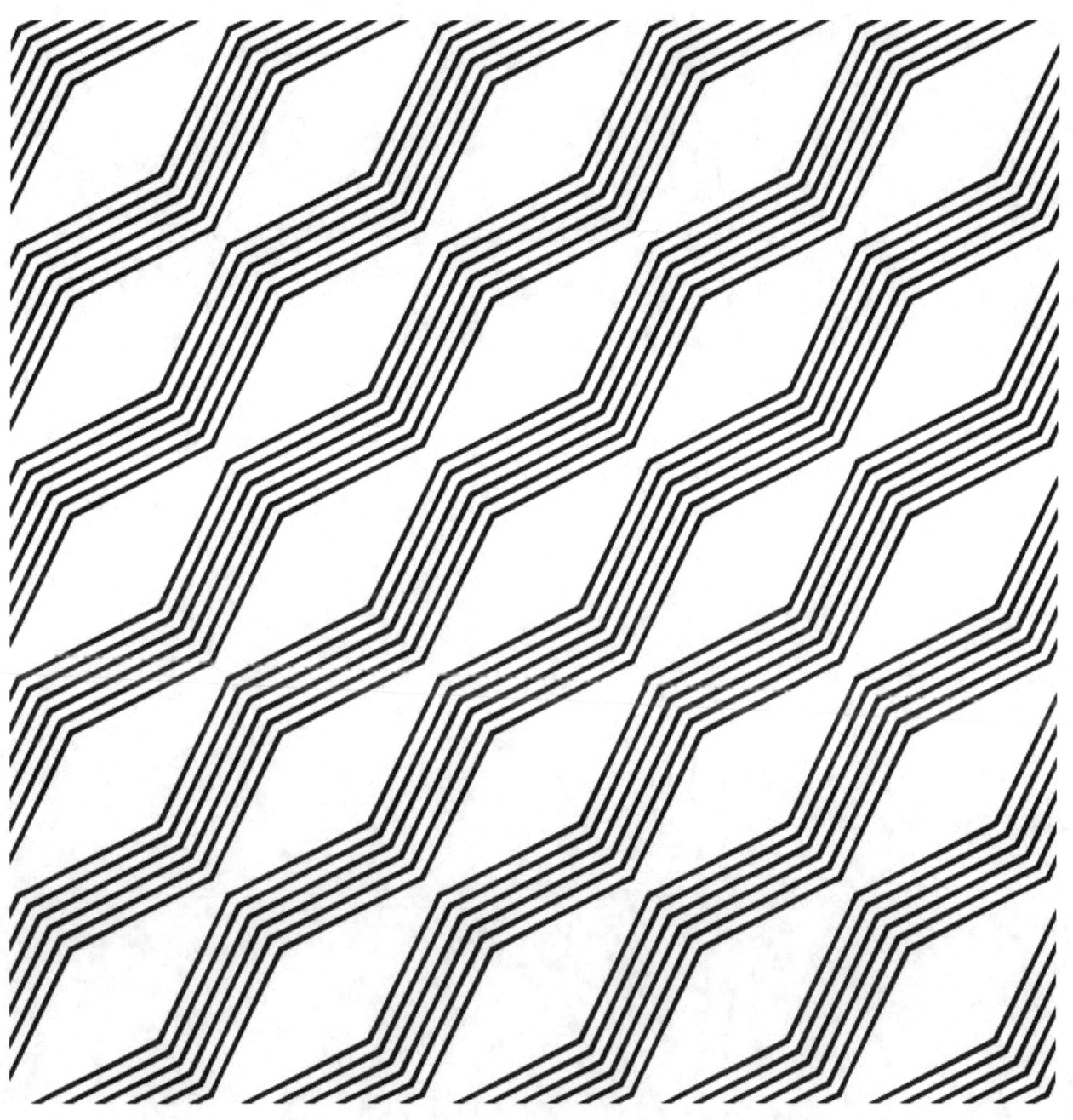

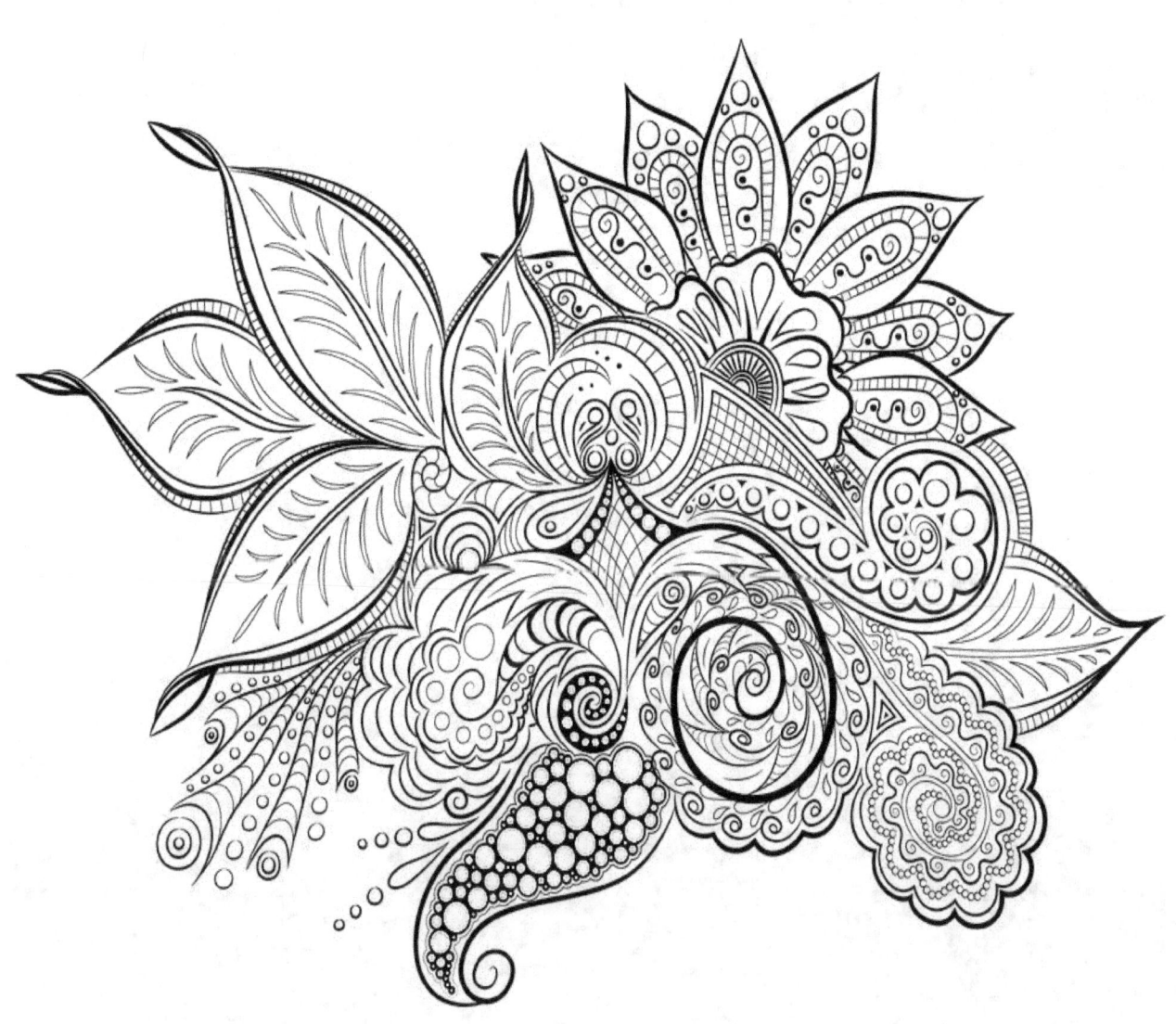

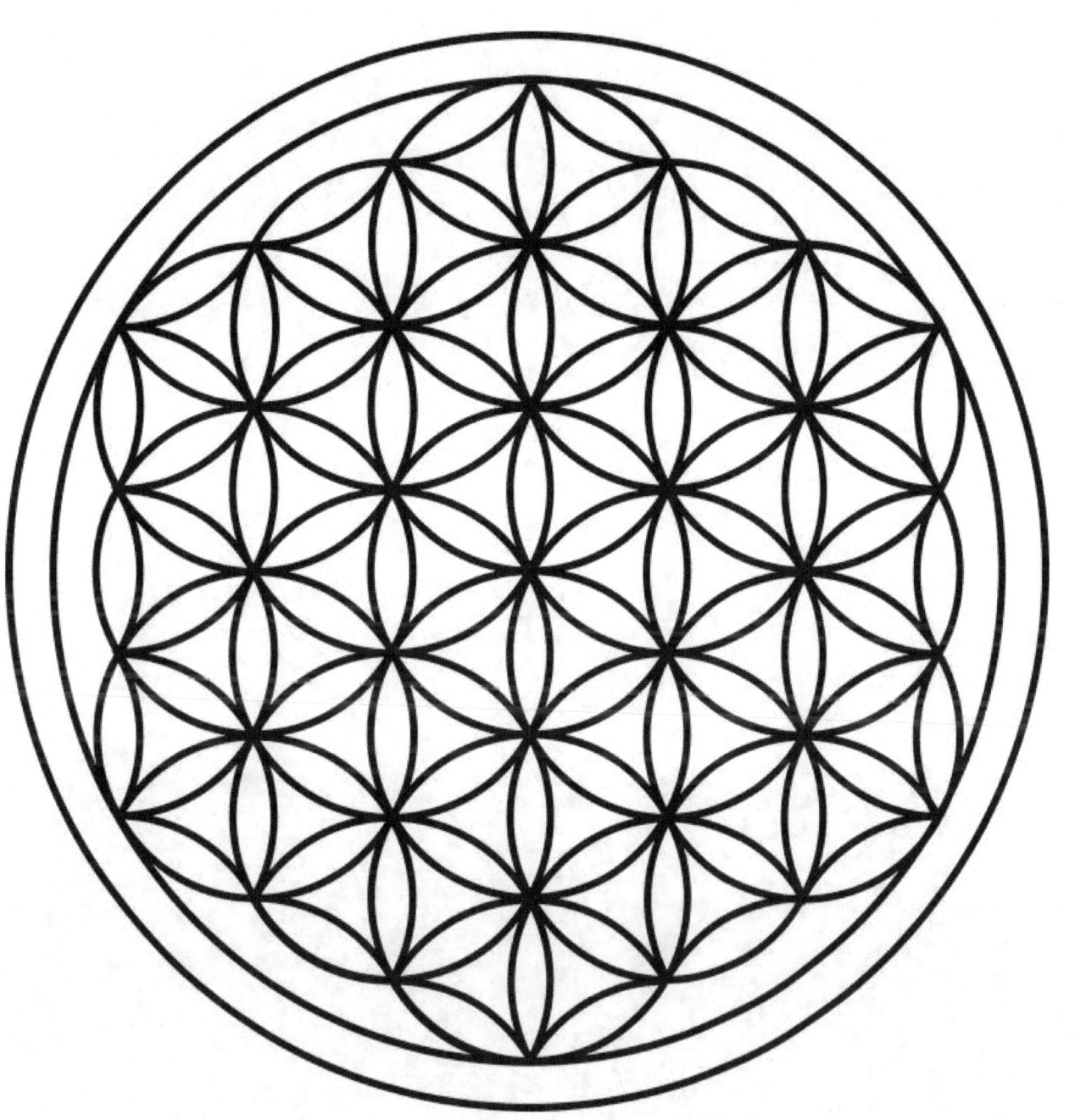

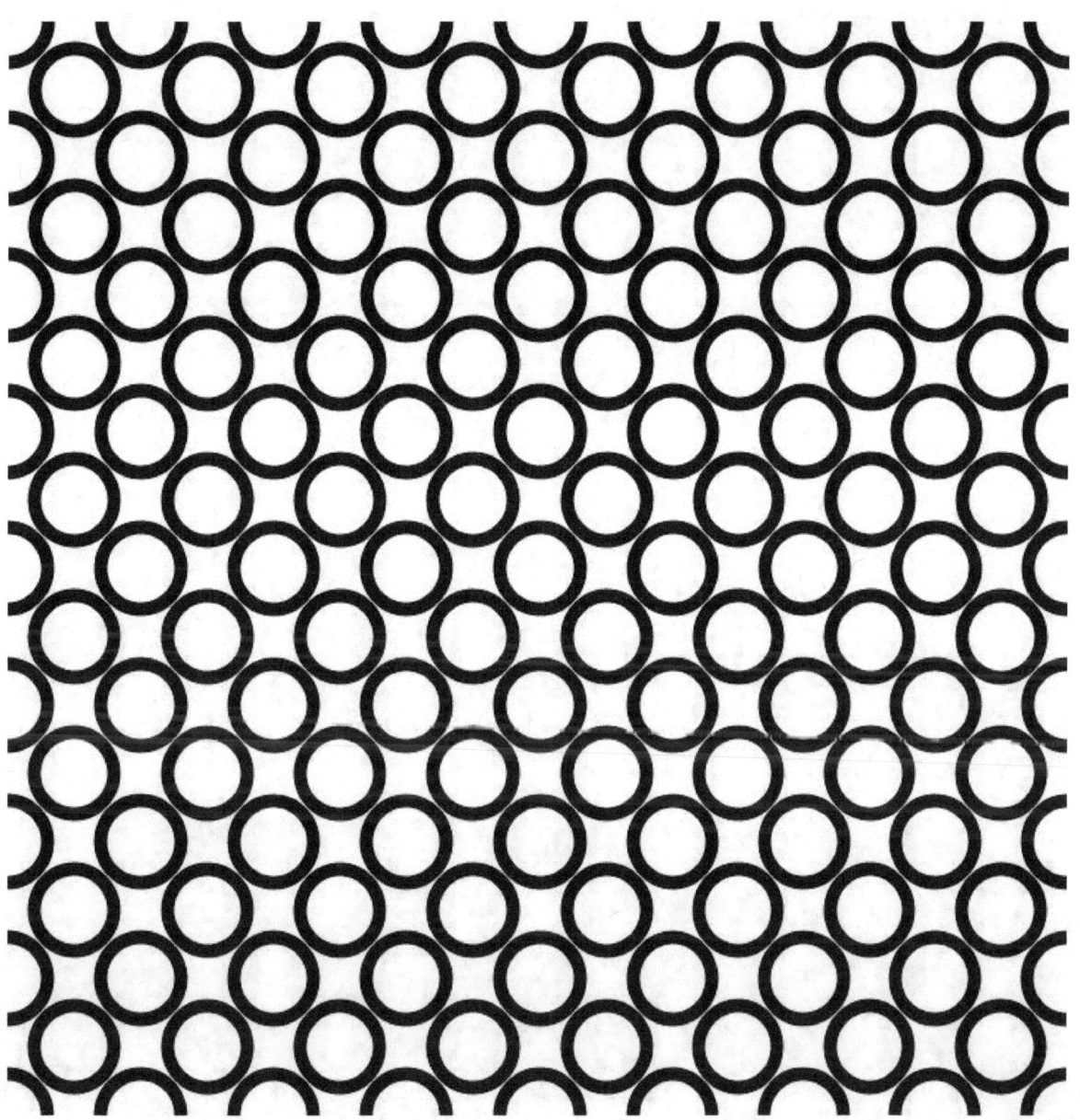

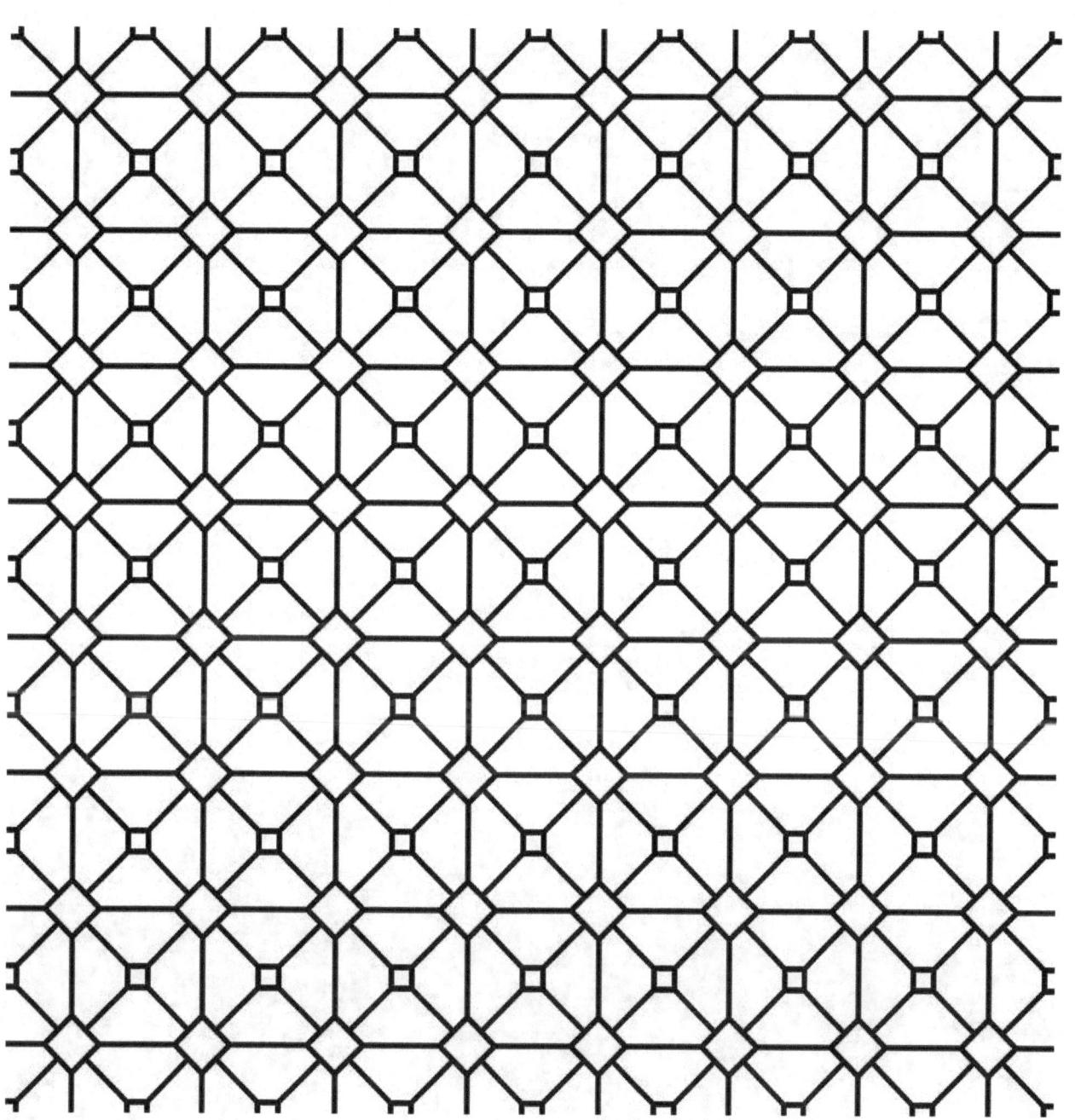

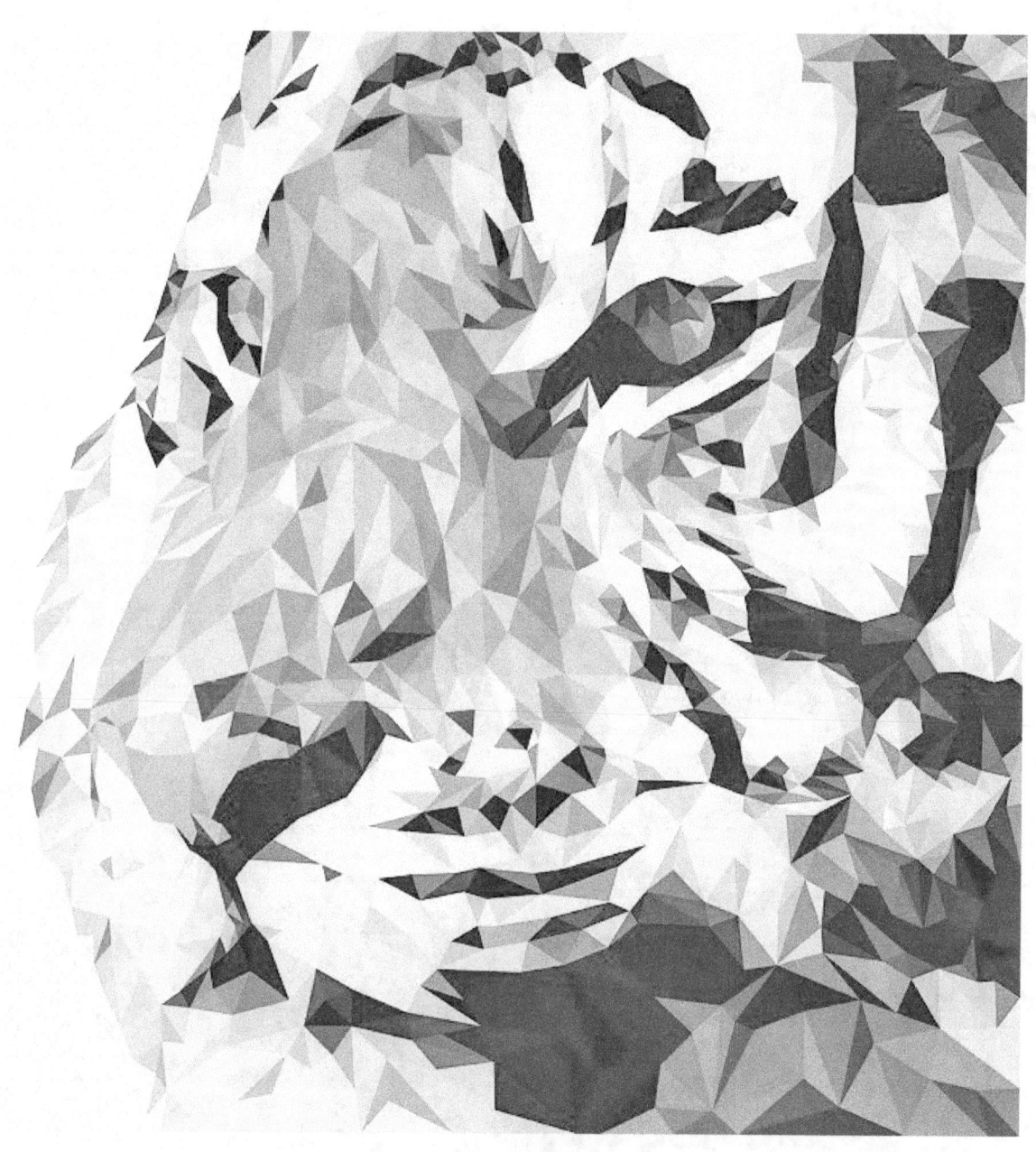

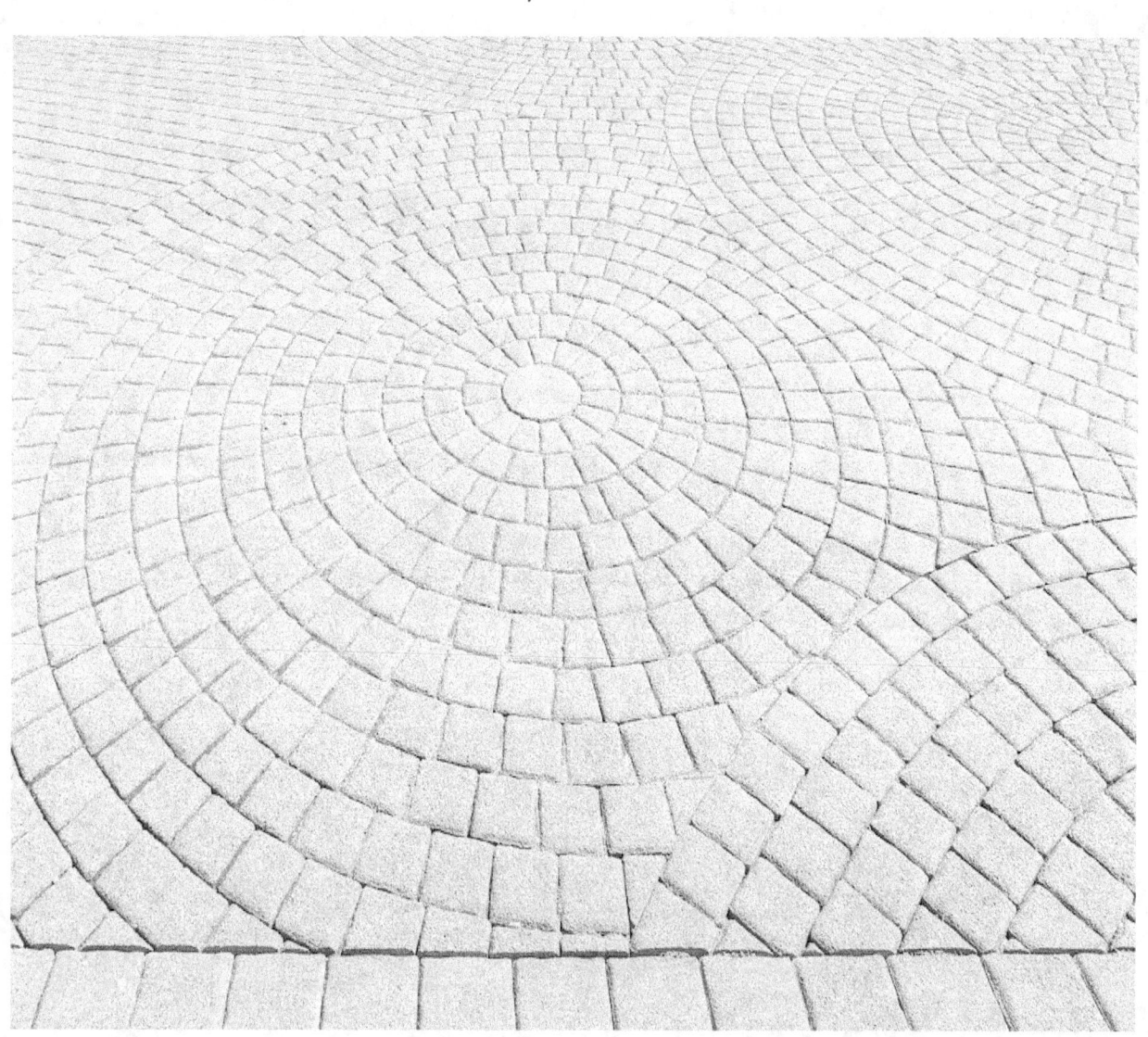

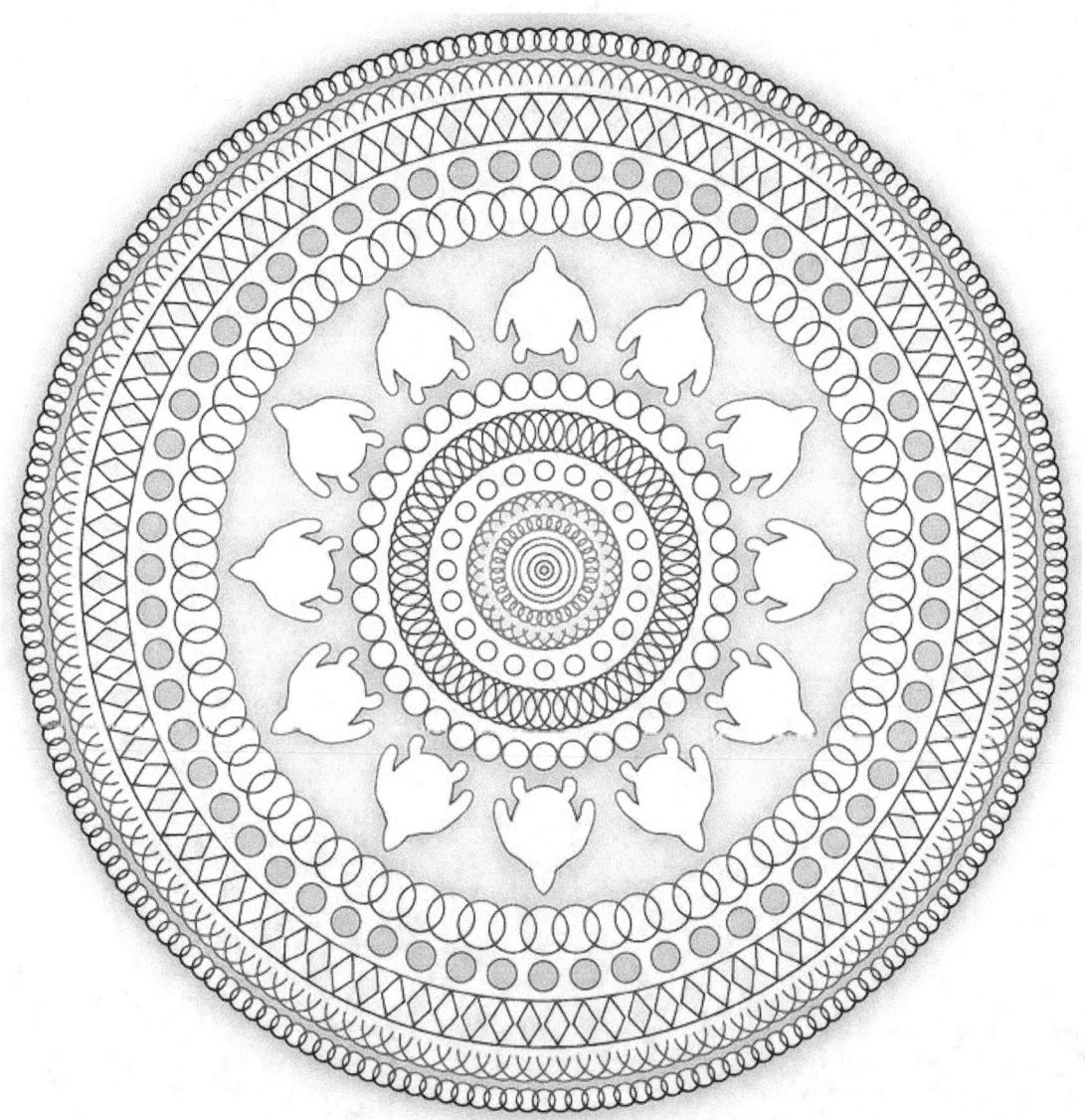

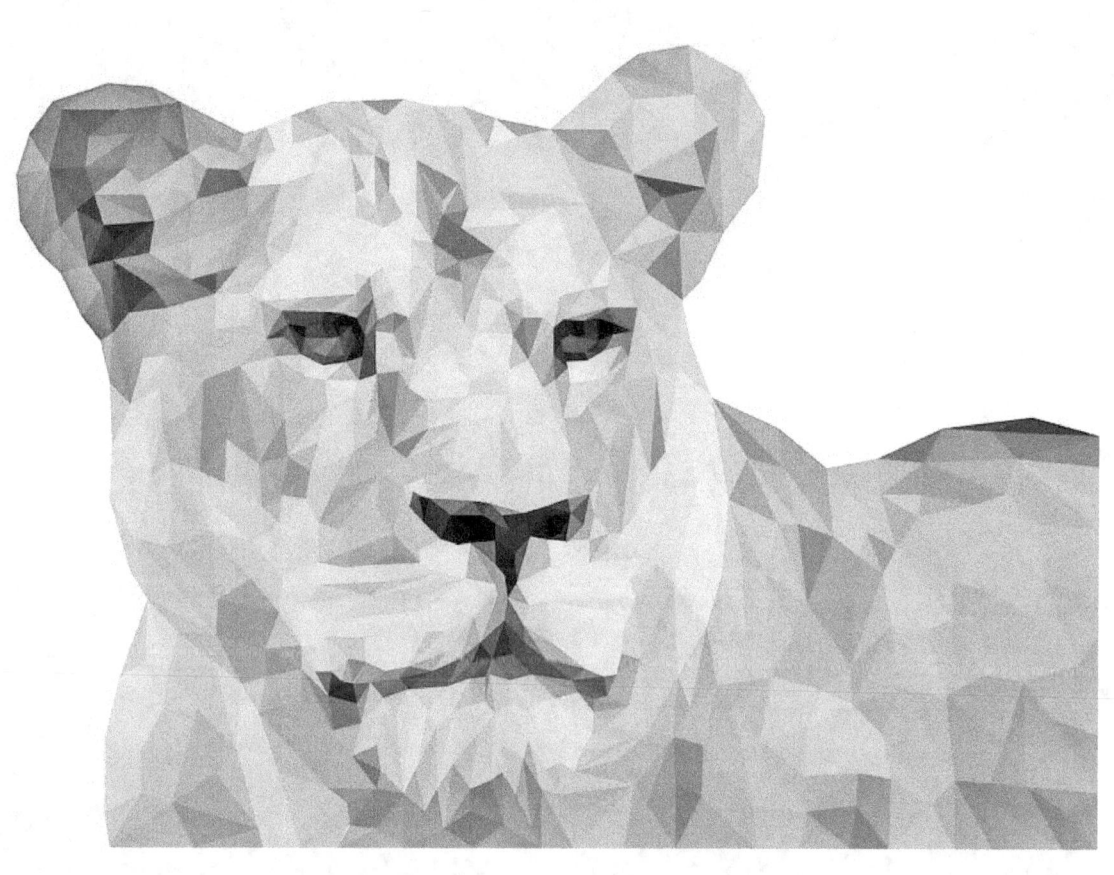

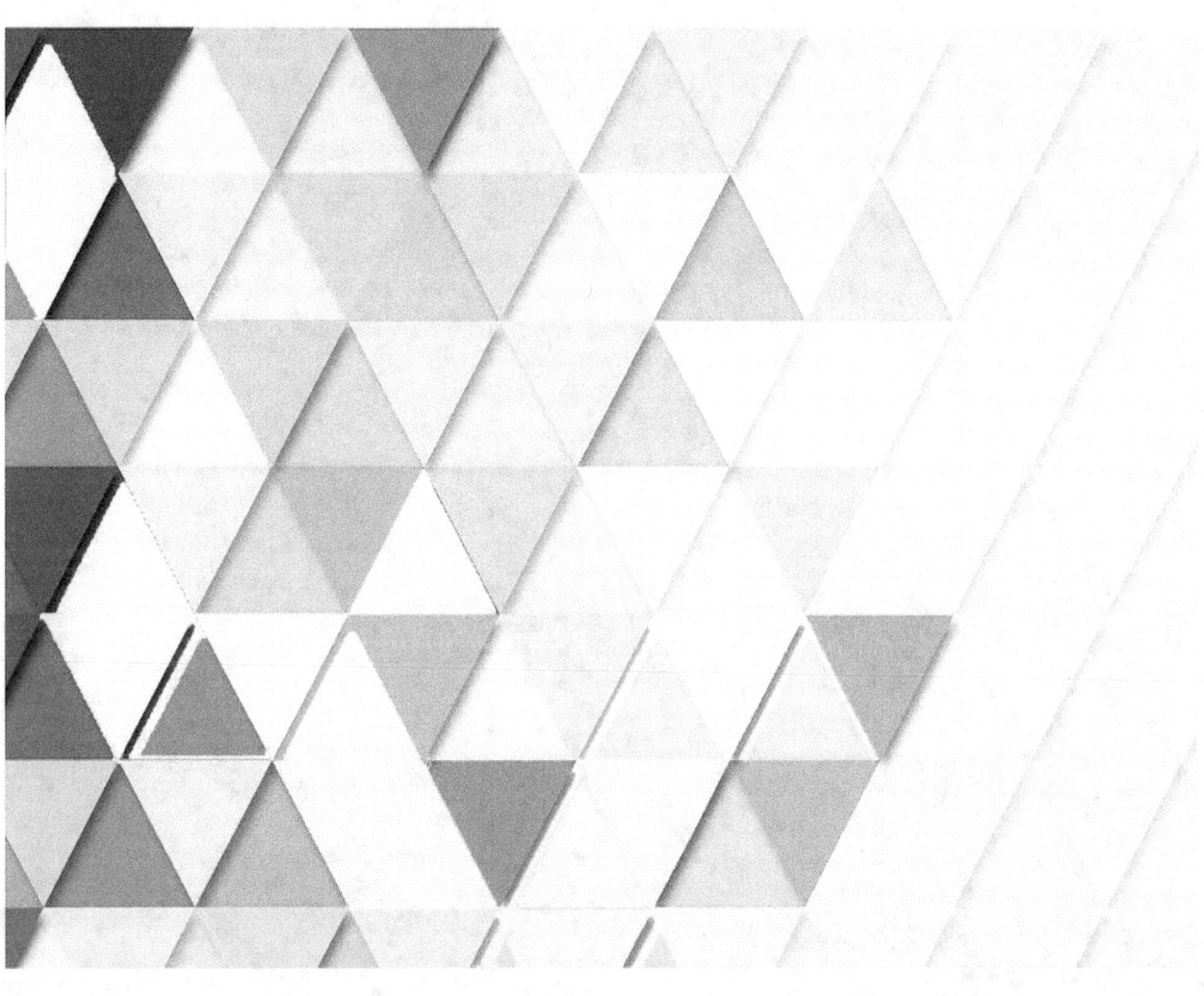

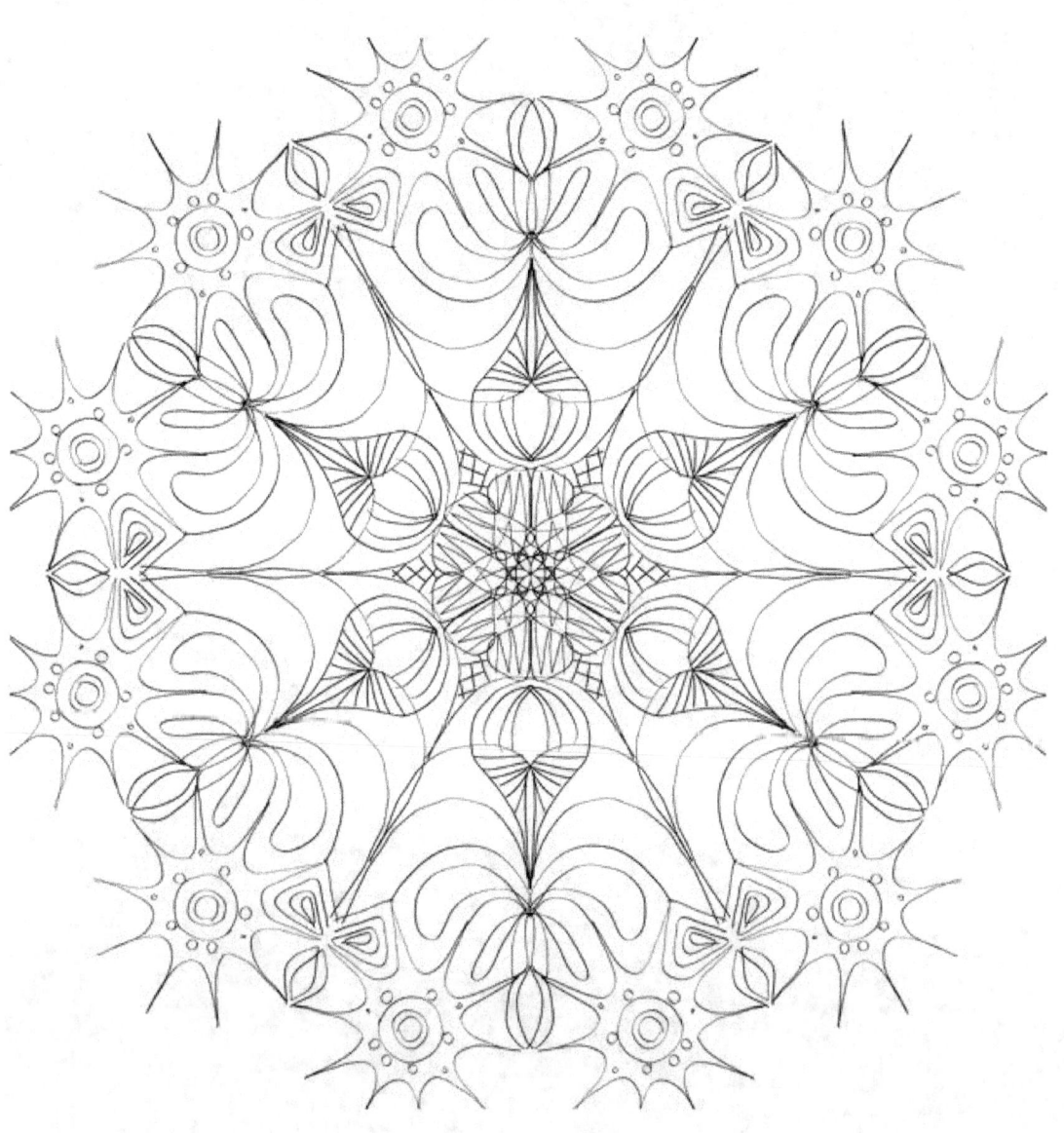

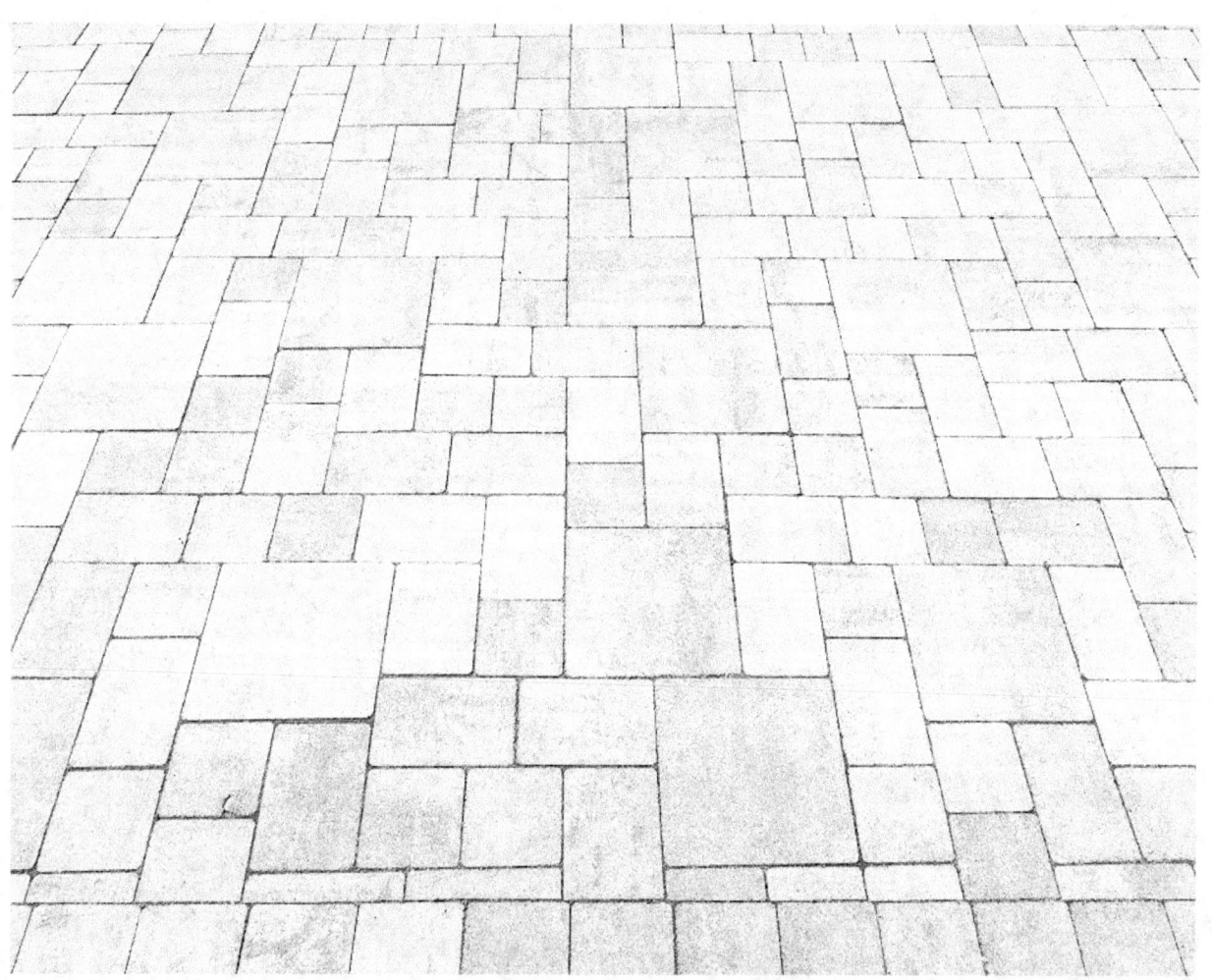

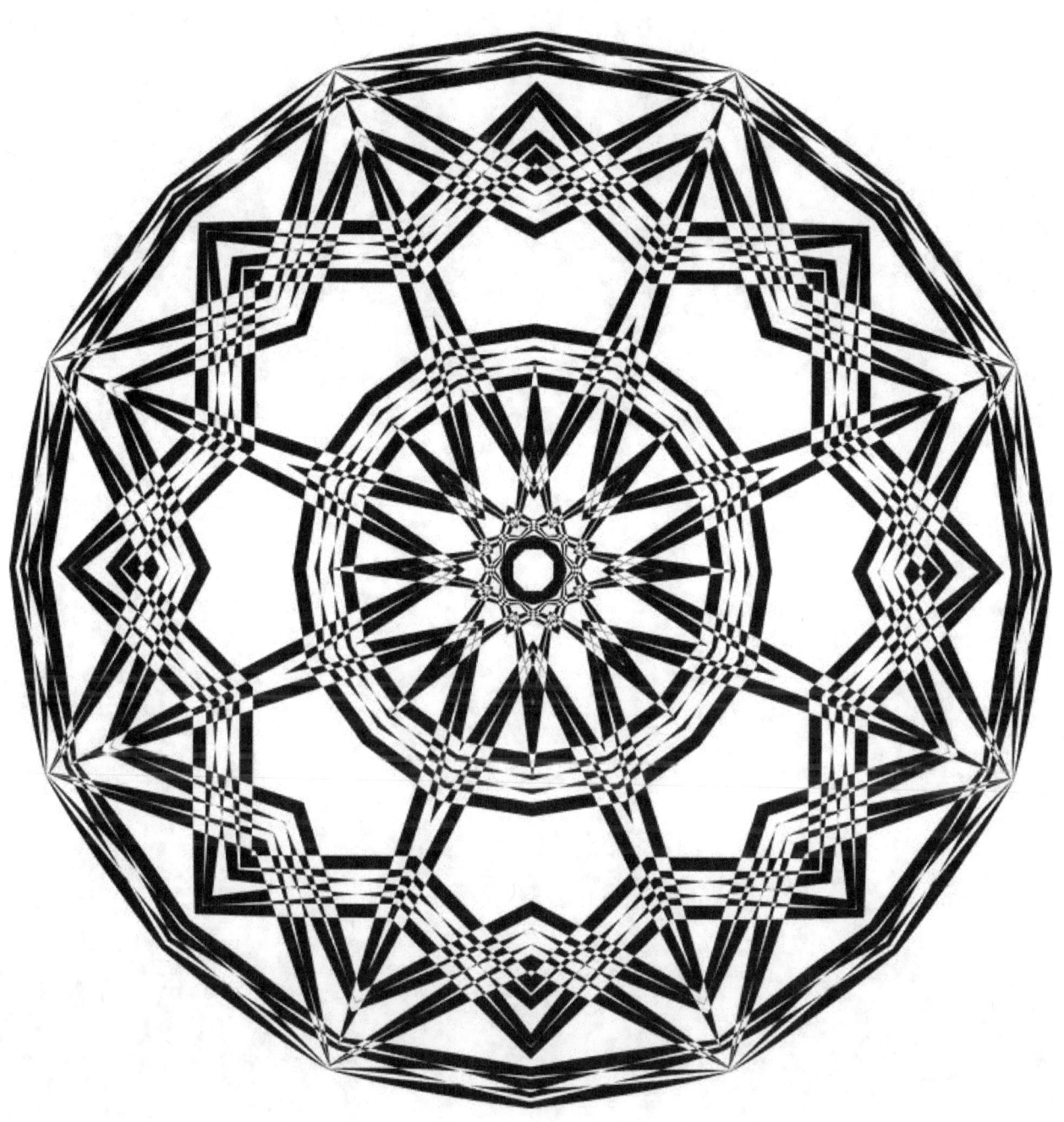

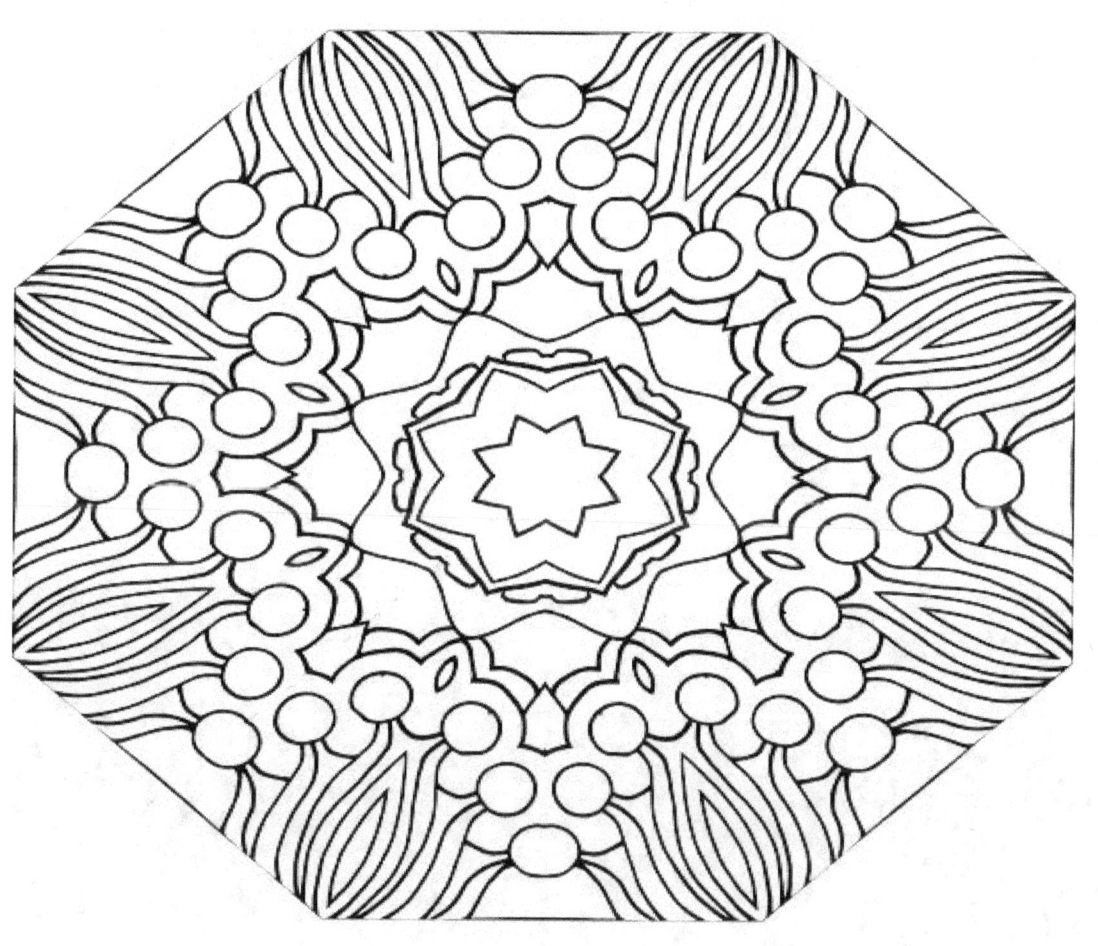

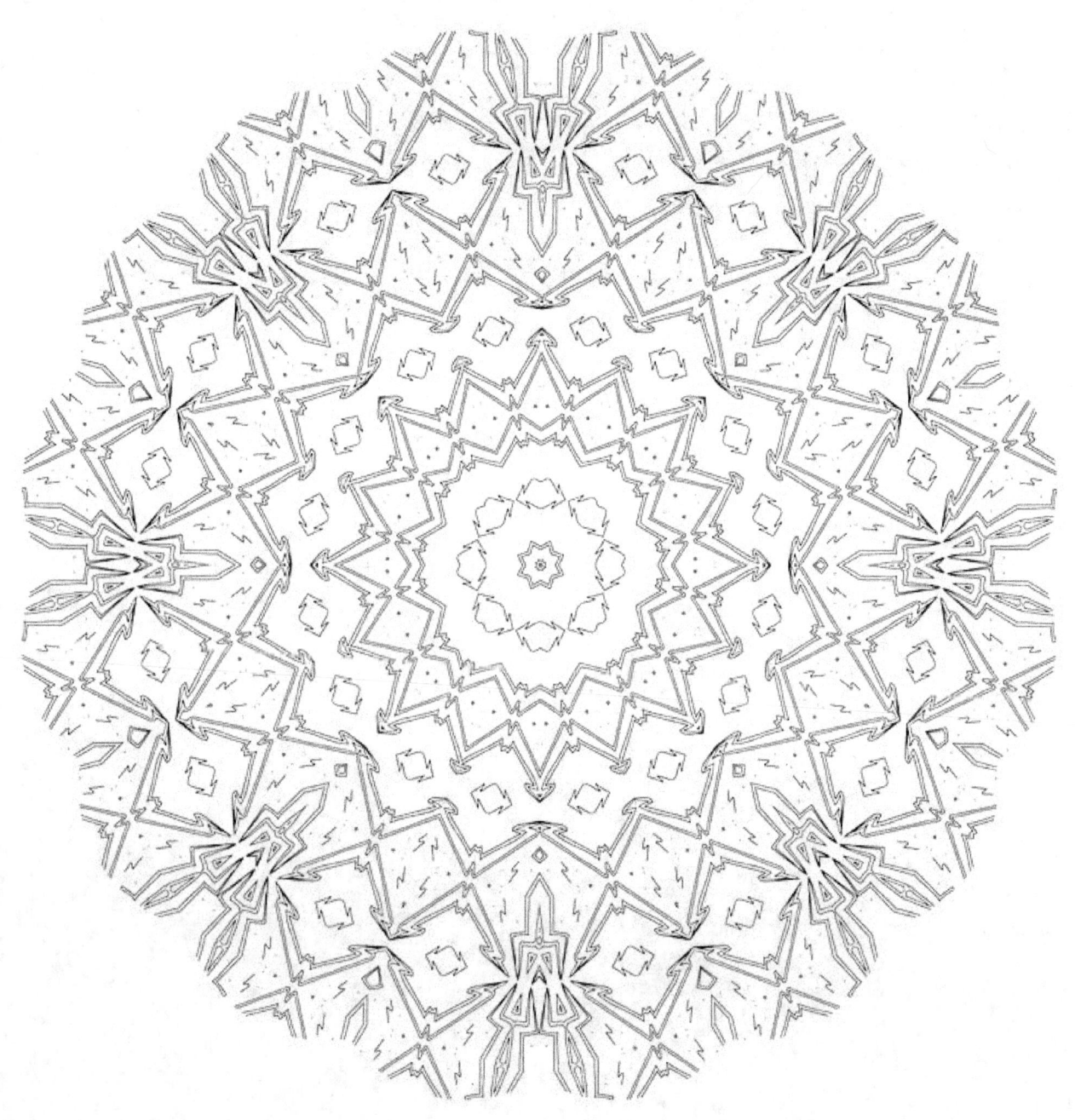

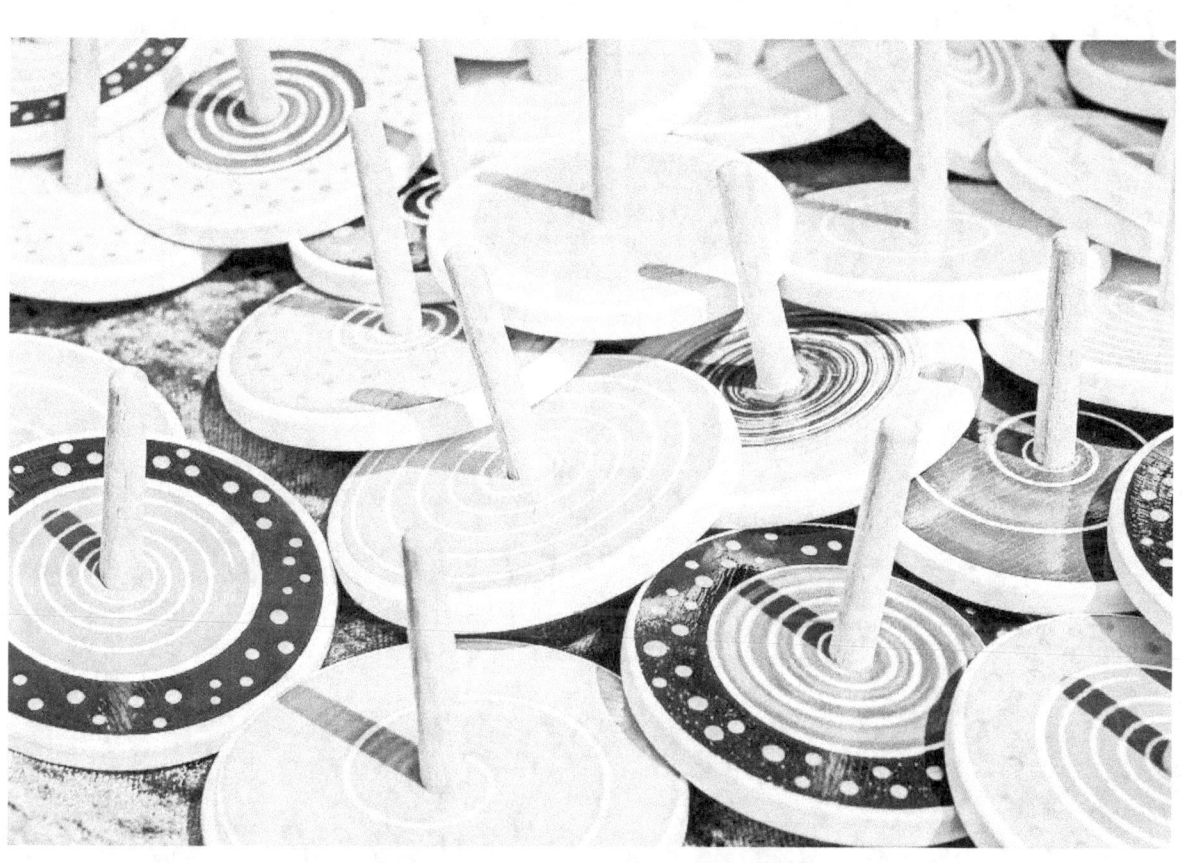

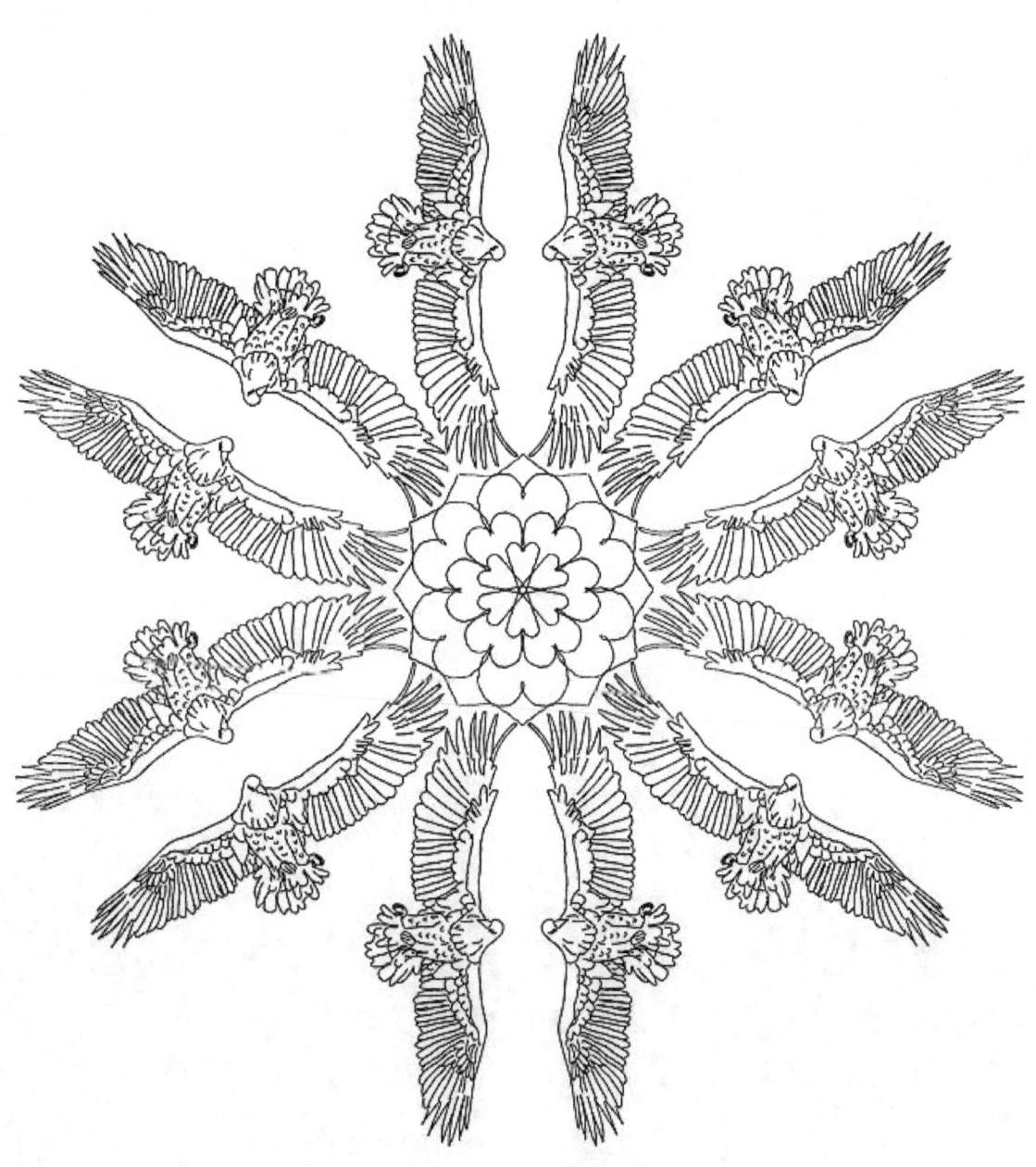

www.ingramcontent.com/pod-product-compliance
Lightning Source LLC
Chambersburg PA
CBHW062219220526
45471CB00009B/3269